Trout Fishing
in the
Black Hills

The Highweather Guide To

Trout Fishing
in the
Black Hills

*A Guide to the Lakes and
Streams of The Black Hills of
South Dakota and Wyoming*

S TEVE K INSELLA

SAINT PAUL, MINNESOTA

The Highweather Press, LLC
Post Office Box 211314
Saint Paul, Minnesota 55121

The Highweather Press publishes fine regional fly-fishing guides. For a complete list, write to the address above.

ISBN 0-9632344-0-4

10 9 8 7 6 5 4 3 2 1 FIRST EDITION

Jacket maps are from the United States Geologic Survey, Savoy and Custer Quadrangles, South Dakota.

Cover design, illustrations and maps by Brad Springer
Front and back cover photographs by Phil Aarrestad
Photograph on page 36 by John van Vliet
All other photographs courtesy South Dakota Tourism

The Highweather Press & Highweather Press logo are trademarks of The Highweather Press, LLC

DEDICATION

To Ann
for her love, understanding
and editing skills.

To my parents, Jack and Audrey Kinsella,
for putting a cane pole in my hand.

And to my late brother Jim,
whose presence I could feel on every stream.

ACKNOWLEDGMENTS

Books like this are huge undertakings that can only be successful with the help, advice and generosity of many people. The names below are just a few of the people who made this book possible and to whom I am forever indebted. I'm sure there are others I mistakenly omitted from the list. If you are one of those people, please accept my apologies.

My sincere thanks to Steve Veverka, John van Vliet, Alan Spaulding, Bruce and Cindy Hermann, Rick Cordes, Dale Daniels, Rich and Tylynn Gordon, Greg Gunderson, Dr. Jack Redden, Whit Fosburgh, Aileen "Ace" Gallagher, Bud Stewart, Kevin Krog, Dunn Brothers Coffee in St. Paul for the great coffee and the use of their electrical outlet, and to Burleigh, my faithful—although at times impatient—camping, fishing and hunting partner.

Contents

FOREWORD

B *lack Hills.* No two words throughout the West stir a greater range of emotions—wonderment, pride, a sense of history, cultural attachment, spiritual attachment, awe and reverence. For the Lakota and the Cheyenne, the Black Hills are a sacred place. It is where they cut their lodge poles, camped in its sheltered valleys in the winter, and where they often buried their dead. For the non-Indian, too, it is a special place, as demonstrated by one statewide voter referendum after another defeating development efforts that threatened to spoil the Black Hills' environment.

Whether it is the steep, winding limestone canyons and waterfalls of the northern Black Hills, the granite spires of the southern Black Hills or the voice of the wind whispering through its forests, wilderness areas and outer grasslands, this ancient mountain range is truly one of the most picturesque and historic places in the United States. It is also home to some of the West's great trout waters—waters that are pristine and uncrowded.

Growing up in South Dakota, my family spent summer vacations in the Black Hills, where I fished for trout with a spinning rod and lure. Later, as a Boy Scout, I hiked and camped 70 miles through the heart of the Black Hills. (Plus a half dozen more after our scoutmaster got us lost.) As an adult, I was fortunate to have had the opportunity to live in the northern Black Hills for several years, during which time I began to learn how to fly fish for trout, exploring further the many streams and canyons. It is a place to which, even today—living more than 600 miles away—I am continually drawn, preferring to spend my time there more than anywhere else.

It is with that respect and admiration that I write this book—so you who are drawn by the lure of the trout and the peaceful beauty of a remote canyon or a mountain meadow can experience its beauty and history. While this book lists trout streams and lakes, access points, tips on fishing the Black Hills and hatch charts, it is also intended to provide a sense of the history and place. I wrote it this way to help you understand that in any given spot, your backcast may cross the piece of ground where the Lakota military leader Crazy Horse was born; the creek where you are wading may be where George Armstrong Custer watered his horses during his exploratory march through the Black Hills; the rock you are standing on, in the cool shadow of a cliff, may be the same rock where a former U. S. president stood, casting for trout, trying to escape the summer heat of Washington and the political heat of the White House. And everywhere you go you will discover incredible natural wonders carved by water, wind and time.

Because a couple of million people visit the Black Hills each year, many with the family fishing rod in the trunk, this book was written with all ages and experience levels in mind. Whether you are an experienced fly angler or the person who fishes once a year on the annual family vacation, the Black Hills offer trout fishing for all skill levels and all interests.

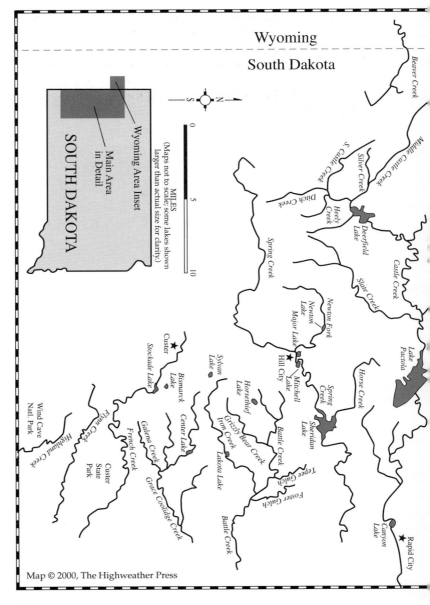

Wyoming

South Dakota

SOUTH DAKOTA

Wyoming Area Inset

Main Area
in Detail

MILES
(Maps not to scale; some lakes shown
larger than actual size for clarity.)

0   5   10

Beaver Creek

Middle Castle Creek

S. Castle Creek

Silver Creek

Ditch Creek

Heely Creek

Deerfield Lake

Castle Creek

Spring Creek

State Creek

Newton Fork

Newton Lake

Major Lake

Lake Pactola

Horse Creek

Spring Creek

Sylvan Lake

Mitchell Lake

Hill City

Horsethief Lake

Sheridan Lake

Custer

Stockade Lake

Bismarck Lake

Center Lake

Grizzly Bear Creek

Iron Creek

Battle Creek

Tepee Gulch

Foster Gulch

Wind Cave Natl. Park

Highland Creek

Flynn Creek

Galena Creek

French Creek

Custer State Park

Grace Coolidge Creek

Lakota Lake

Battle Creek

Canyon Lake

Rapid City

Map © 2000, The Highweather Press

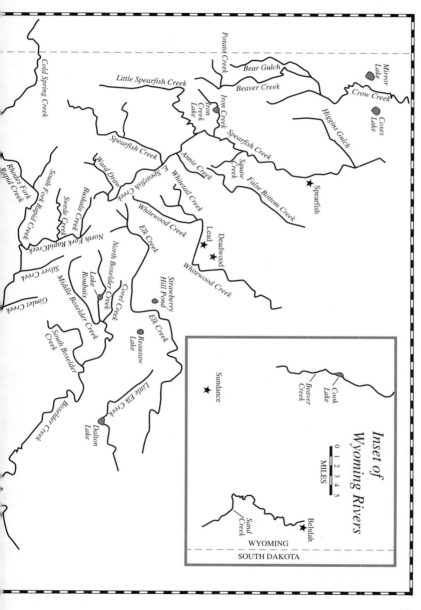

15

Part 1

The Black Hills

Harney Peak, the highest point in the central United States east of the Rocky Mountains, towers over Sylvan Lake.

THE BLACK HILLS

GEOLOGY AND GEOGRAPHY OF THE BLACK HILLS

One hundred miles long, roughly forty miles wide and saddling the border of two states and including the Bear Lodge Mountains of Wyoming, the Black Hills are comprised of some of the oldest geological formations in North America. The central part of the Black Hills is made up of igneous and metamorphic rocks ranging from 1.7 billion to more than 2.5 billion years old. These old rocks are the remnants of several ancient mountain ranges long since destroyed by time and the forces of nature. Most of the outer parts of the Black Hills are composed of sedimentary rocks ranging from about 60 million years to over 500 million years old.

Until about 58 million years ago, these sedimentary deposits overlaid the older rock formations. However, the uplifting—or *doming*—of the central Black Hills led to erosion which eventually removed the younger sedimentary rock. At the end of this period of erosion, roughly 38 million years ago, the Black Hills actually looked very much as they do today. The eroded material, combined with volcanic ash from the western United States, produced the Badlands to the east of the Black Hills.

There are three distinct and unique ecological regions within the Black Hills. These include: the *foothills*, which are made up of soft red siltstones, sandstones and shales and are characterized by spotted growths of pine woodlands and grasses; the *high plateau*, largely comprised of limestone and characterized by limestone canyons, grass and pine covered valleys and relatively level pine forests; and the *central core highlands*, made up of granite, schist and quartzite, and generally rugged and covered by ponderosa pine. In the southern part of the core highlands, near Custer and Mt. Rushmore, there are steep, jagged peaks of granite. The most distinguished feature of this region is Harney Peak, which at 7,242 feet is the highest mountain in the United States east of the Rocky Mountains.

Two prominent features of the Black Hills are the Hogback and the Red Valley, which is often referred to as "the Racetrack." The Hogback consists of erosion-resistant sandstone, which forms a ridge extending around the outer Black Hills. The Red Valley lies within this ridge and is comprised of soft red shale and siltstone. It can be seen most clearly when driving through it on Interstate 90 on the way from Rapid City to Spearfish. One of the legends of the Lakota Indians (the proper name for the people commonly referred to as the Sioux) is that the Black Hills and the Red

Valley were created when a multitude of animals on earth began racing furiously in a great circle. The race lasted for days and ended when the earth heaved up at the center of the race and spewed ash and lava on the animals, killing them. The legend says the Red Valley is what remains of the racetrack.

The Black Hills are comprised of a unique spectrum of minerals, including gold and other precious minerals. The largest-producing gold mine in the Americas, known as the Homestake—originally developed by the Hearst family—is in the northern Black Hills. Sparkling feldspar and quartzite are abundant along roads and on the mountainsides in the southern part of the region. Agates can be found in many of its streams. The fact that the geological formations of the Black Hills are exposed and easily accessible is why every summer vanloads of geology students from across the United States can be seen throughout the area studying its features.

The Black Hills are also home to many other important geological features. There are waterfalls in the northern Black Hills, and caves throughout the regions underlain by limestone. One of the most unique caves is Wind Cave, a national park in the southern Black Hills. Since its discovery in the late 1800s, nearly 80 miles have been mapped. Park officials estimate that those discoveries constitute less than 10 percent of the total area of the cave.

The geological and physical features of the Black Hills, and particularly the presence of limestone in the plateau region and as a band encircling the Hills, are the reason its creeks are so well-suited for trout. The Hills squeeze precious moisture out of the prevailing zonal weather flows— far more than the region immediately surrounding the Hills receives—while the porous limestone continually recharges the underlying aquifer with the increased amount of rain and snowfall. This, in turn, produces the springs that provide the creeks with a life-giving source of cold, clean water that flows consistently throughout the year. It is not uncommon in the Black Hills to have a half dozen or more springs in a few square miles feeding a creek. In addition, the limestone substrate helps keep a stream's pH at levels ideal for the survival and production of trout, as well as the insects and other aquatic foods on which they feed.

BLACK HILLS HISTORY

The Black Hills played a critical role in the histories of Native Americans and the American West. Open any history book that focuses on the American West and you will see repeated references to the Black Hills and how this region changed the lives of individuals and influenced the course of cultures. The existence of the Black Hills and what they meant to Indian and non-Indian cultures alike, was a key factor that led to the war in the second half of the nineteenth century between the Lakota and Cheyenne and the United States government.

Humans first came into contact with the Black Hills when small nomadic bands of Paleo-Indian hunters ventured into the region shortly after the Ice Age. Later, the Kiowa, Crow and other tribes made the Black Hills their home, but they were forced out in the 1700s by the militarily superior Lakota who were themselves being pushed westward from what is now Minnesota and Wisconsin.

The Lakota call the Black Hills "Paha Sapa," or "black mountains," because, from a distance, the pines give the mountains a dark appearance—a striking contrast to the lighter, muted colors of the surrounding treeless plains. For the Cheyenne and Lakota, the Black Hills are considered sacred and are the center of their respective universes and religions. The Lakota refer to the Black Hills as the "heart of everything that is." For the Cheyenne it was on a mountain adjacent to the northern Black Hills—known as Bear Butte—

near present-day Sturgis, where their religion and traditions originated, and where they received the four sacred arrows that have guided their culture through time. On that same mountain, the Lakota, including leaders like Crazy Horse, Sitting Bull and Red Cloud, received the sacred visions that guided their lives.

In addition to being central to their beliefs, the Black Hills provided many Lakota and Cheyenne with lodge poles for their tepees. Here, too, they sought the shelter and mild climate of the Black Hills, spending winters in its valleys. There were tribal gatherings held nearby, including the famous 1857 gathering during which many bands from the Lakota nation came together near Bear Butte. It was during this gathering that the Lakota made the decision to stop the advances of the whites into their sacred territory.

Historians believe the first non-Indians to see the Black Hills were the French explorers, the La Verendrye brothers, on New Year's Day in 1743 during their unsuccessful quest to discover a route to the Pacific Ocean. Lewis and Clark learned of the existence of the Black Hills in 1803 from a French trapper they met during their famous exploratory expedition up the Missouri River and to the Pacific Ocean. But it was more than a hundred years after the Verendrye brothers' sighting that the Hills were first fully explored by non-Indians. It was not until 1874, when a brash young Colonel named George Armstrong Custer led more than one thousand soldiers, 110 wagons, 300 cattle, a handful of miners and journalists, and a marching band from Ft. Abraham Lincoln (near present day Bismarck, North Dakota), to and through the heart of the Black Hills and back again.

The purpose of Custer's mission was to explore the region and send back detailed information to his superiors in Washington concerning the character of the Black Hills. He was there also to demonstrate a show of force to the

Lakota and the Cheyenne and to scout a possible location for a military fort. As he entered the Black Hills from what is now Wyoming, the Lakota set the prairies around him on fire and constantly shadowed his progress. At night, the Lakota campfires were visible to Custer and his men—an eery foreshadowing of his later fate.

Custer used adjectives like *exquisite, luxuriant, beautiful* and *enchanting* to describe the Black Hills. Fortunately for historians, he brought with him a young photographer from St. Paul, Minnesota, named William H. Illingworth who took over 70 photographs of the unique geological features they passed during the exploration, including a number of present-day trout streams. Illingworth's images were the first photographs ever taken of the Black Hills and the stereophotographic glass plates are in the possession of the South Dakota State Historical Society. Stereophotos from the plates are currently on display at the Journey Museum in Rapid City.

Custer's exploration also resulted in a discovery that would change the Black Hills forever. Gold was discovered in a small creek in the southern Black Hills by gold panners accompanying Custer. The reports that circulated back from the expedition to the eastern United States and the West Coast were that gold was literally clinging to the roots of the grass in the Black Hills. One newspaper even went as far as to report that the national debt would be paid off shortly after Custer's return, thanks to the Black Hills gold discovery. As was so typical of the day, those reports were highly exaggerated. In fact a geologist who accompanied the Custer expedition gave the gold reports "a large grain of disallowance."

After Custer's reports of gold, fortune seekers, including the likes of James Butler "Wild Bill" Hickok, soon poured into the Black Hills. They established makeshift mining camps which took the names of Deadwood, Custer, Hill City and Rockerville. The Lakota and Cheyenne were outraged. Under the Ft. Laramie Treaty signed in 1868, they had sole possession of what is now western South Dakota and portions of eastern Wyoming and Montana, as well as the Black Hills. In signing the treaty giving them possession of these lands ". . . for as long as the grass will grow, and the waters flow. . ." the Lakota and Cheyenne had given away large tracts of their historical land holdings in other parts of the West. Now it looked as though the United States government was going to take their most sacred land holding of all—the Black Hills.

Skirmishes and battles broke out between the Indians, settlers and the U.S. military, culminating in 1876 with the annihilation of Custer and more than two hundred soldiers under his command along a small river in Montana known as the Little Big Horn. Fourteen years later, in the shadow of the Black Hills, the United States government retaliated when a battery of Hotchkiss guns massacred more than 300 Lakota men, women and children at a place called Wounded Knee. Wounded Knee marked the end of efforts by the Plains Indians to retain control of the region and total independence from the United States government.*

As the tint of gold mining in the Black Hills began to dim in the late 1800s, and gold miners went elsewhere in search of fortunes, regional promoters started to look for new economic vehicles to promote the Black Hills. One of those vehicles was tourism and a recreational sport that was growing in popularity—trout fishing. Trout stocking and trout fishing had become the rage throughout the United States. The Black Hills and their cold, crystal-clear creeks became a perfect location for establishing a thriving trout fishery.

---

* Today the Lakota still claim ownership of the Black Hills, citing the broken Ft. Laramie Treaty of 1868. In the 1980s, the U.S. Supreme Court ruled that the United States government must pay the Lakota millions of dollars for illegally seizing the Black Hills. In spite of the damage award, the Lakota still refuse to cede the Black Hills. The damage award, which with interest has grown into a mountain of money of sorts, has gone untouched.

HISTORY OF TROUT IN THE BLACK HILLS

The first documented reference to fishing in the Black Hills came during Custer's 1874 reconnaissance. A newspaper correspondent wrote that, as they were leaving the Black Hills, they camped near a stream with, "sufficient fish to supply the entire camp." (The stream he was referring to was probably Boxelder Creek, today a popular trout stream.) However, it is likely they were not fishing for trout but rather suckers or chubs. Because of its isolated location away from regions that contained natural trout populations, and the fact that the warm rivers that surround the Black Hills were not suitable for trout propagation and survival, trout had to be introduced into the Black Hills.

According to historians, trout were first brought to the Black Hills in 1886 by Richard Hughes, a former gold miner turned journalist, and Samuel Scott, one of Rapid City's founders. The two believed the Black Hills and its streams would make perfect trout habitat, which, in turn, would help develop the region's tourism potential. They arranged for a shipment of trout from Colorado via stagecoach and then planted those trout in Rapid Creek and Cleghorn Springs west of Rapid City.

At roughly the same time and into the 1890s, government biologists began researching the Black Hills to determine its potential as trout habitat. They noted that, "despite abundance of fresh water shrimp and other good trout food in the pure spring water, we are surprised there are no trout native to Black Hills streams."[*] In 1891, the United States Fish Commission began to experiment with trout propagation in the Black Hills by planting brook trout near Rapid City and in Spearfish Creek. Though transporting the fish into the Black Hills was difficult and survival rates low, those surviving trout flourished.

Seeing the potential for trout production in the Black

---

[*] Report of the U.S. Fish Commission Investigation Team, 1892

Hills, the United States government in the late 1890s authorized the construction of what they called a "fish cultural station"—now more commonly referred to as a hatchery. The Government chose Spearfish as the location for the hatchery and by July of 1899, approximately 100,000 trout eggs were incubating at what became known as the Spearfish National Fish Hatchery. In 1900, 25,000 brook trout were stocked in Whitewood Creek and Little Spearfish Creek, and that same year, "black-spotted trout," or cutthroat trout, were stocked in Iron Creek and Spearfish Creek. The next year, Loch Leven brown trout were stocked in Boxelder Creek and rainbow trout were stocked in Iron Creek and Spearfish Creek. By the time the United States entered World War I, the Black Hills had become famous nationally, not only for its beauty, but also as a developing trout-fishing destination.

The Spearfish National Fish Hatchery was eventually renamed to honor its first superintendent, D.C. Booth. During its heyday, the hatchery propagated and stocked brook, rainbow and brown trout, as well as steelhead, lake trout and Atlantic salmon for other regions of the nation. In the early days of the hatchery's operation, it was responsible for trout propagation throughout the West and operated a "black-spotted trout" egg-gathering station in Yellowstone National Park.

Not surprisingly, the isolated location of the Black Hills required the development of creative transportation systems for the highly fragile trout and eggs. Fish-carrying rail cars were created out of converted baggage and passenger cars. The cars were first stripped and then refitted with fish tanks. Mechanical and electrical air pumps were installed to provide oxygen for the trout, and the tanks then surrounded with ice to keep the water cold during the frequently long, slow trip to the streams.

The D.C. Booth hatchery operated until 1983. It was restored in the early 1990s and became a historic trout fisheries archive center. Today, the hatchery continues to operate in limited capacity in conjunction with the McNenny Hatchery located a few miles west of Spearfish, and is listed on the National Register of Historic Places.

By the 1930s and 1940s, the Black Hills had become well known as a fishing tourism center, much as Hughes and Scott had planned more than 50 years earlier. Souvenir books from that period encouraged visitors to fish in the "flashing streams" of the Black Hills. One of the first tourism maps of the Black Hills, currently on display at the Lake Pactola visitors center, noted places to fish including Rapid Canyon, Rapid Creek, Spearfish Creek, French Creek and other places that remain popular to this day.

TROUT IN THE BLACK HILLS TODAY

Today, there are approximately 670 miles of trout streams in the Black Hills of South Dakota and approximately 75 miles in the Black Hills of Wyoming, many with naturally reproducing populations of wild trout. The streams range from tiny creeks abundant with wild brook trout to larger streams with sections of wild brown and rainbow trout, as well as brook trout. In addition, Black Hills lakes are stocked regularly with rainbow trout in the 8- to 10-inch range and, in some cases, fingerlings.

The vast majority of streams in the Black Hills are managed for wild brown and brook trout. Officials with the South Dakota Department of Game, Fish and Parks and the Wyoming Game and Fish Department oversee this responsibility and view the raising and stocking of trout as a secondary tool. Their primary tool for the management of Black Hills streams is the protection, restoration and enhancement of existing trout habitat.

Decisions to stock streams, as well as the level of those stockings and the size of the trout stocked, are based on whether natural reproduction occurs in a particular stream and if that level of reproduction meets current fishing demands. Because of abundant self-sustaining populations of wild brook trout, they are no longer stocked in the Black Hills. Both South Dakota and Wyoming have in place trout management plans and continually monitor creeks and lakes throughout the region by conducting fish surveys.

Improvements designed to enhance trout habitat and production have been made on many Black Hills streams in recent years. In South Dakota, many of the improvements are cooperative ventures undertaken by the South Dakota Department of Game, Fish and Parks, the United States Forest Service and the Black Hills Fly-Fishers, a local fly-fishing club dedicated to improving the quality of trout waters. The South Dakota Department of Game, Fish and Parks operates a fish health lab at McNenny Hatchery near Spearfish. The purpose of the lab is to screen the trout at the hatchery for disease-causing agents, to prevent outbreaks such as whirling disease.

There are a number of creeks in the Black Hills that have special regulations in place. For example, some creeks have catch-and-release-only sections designed to improve and enhance populations of wild trout. In addition, to help sustain populations of mature, naturally reproducing trout or to expand the number of trophy-sized fish, other stream sections have limits on the number of trout that can be taken over a certain size. Some of the small lakes also have special regulations in place limiting the number of trout that can be taken above a certain size due to the fact those lakes are stocked, in part, with a population of larger trout, usually in the 16-inch range. Signs are posted at or near the waters where these and other special regulations are in effect. The South Dakota and Wyoming fishing handbooks, available at most fishing shops and sporting goods stores, also list special regulation sections of streams and waters in the Black Hills.

CLIMATE OF THE BLACK HILLS

Moderate temperatures are the mark of the Black Hills. Because of the rugged mountainous topography, temperatures, rainfall and snowfall amounts can vary dramatically from lower elevations, such as Rapid City or Spearfish, to higher elevations, such as Lead and Deadwood or Deerfield and Pactola Lakes. Overall, average spring and summer temperatures range from highs in the mid to upper 50s and lows in the upper 20s and low 30s in April, highs in the low to upper 70s and lows in the upper 40s and low 50s in June, and highs in the 70s and 80s and lows in the 50s in August.

May and June are the wettest months of the year with the Black Hills receiving over a third of its annual rainfall in those two months. On average, August and September are the driest, with Rapid City receiving an average of less than two inches of rain in August. March is generally the snowiest month of the year with an average of 15 to 25 inches in the northern Black Hills and 8 to 12 inches in the southern Hills. Overall, the Rapid City area receives an average of 36 inches of snow and 17 inches of rain each year.

What makes the climate of the Black Hills particularly unique is its winters. Winters in the Black Hills are not what you would expect for the region. Unlike the rugged plains of South Dakota and North Dakota, where sub-zero winter temperatures and flesh-freezing windchills are the norm, the Black Hills have a winter climate more like that of portions of Missouri. This unique climate, caused by the mass of the Black Hills diverting arctic airmasses, and by the warming and drying effect that occurs when cold air is forced up and over the hills (called "Chinook" winds), has earned the Black Hills the nickname of "the banana belt."

What this unusually moderate climate means for the trout fisherman is relatively mild winters with long stretches of days with the temperature in the 40s, often soaring into the 60s. In other words, mid-winter insect hatches, ice-free line guides on your fishing rod and shirt-sleeve fishing—and even sunburn—in February.

The trout seasons in South Dakota and Wyoming run year-round, making it possible to fish throughout the winter, weather permitting. And many Black Hills streams, including sections of Castle Creek, Spring Creek, Rapid Creek, Sand Creek and Spearfish Creek, are frequently fishable all winter. There are also sections below some of the dams, including Lake Pactola, where the release of water combined with the moderate winters usually keep those stretches mostly free of ice in all but the harshest weather.

However, mild winter temperatures in the Black Hills are also unreliable—and even less predictable—so don't make your airline and hotel reservations for a February fishing expedition in August. In a typical February, it can be 60°F one week, but in the grips of a raging blizzard the next. In addition, many of the lodging facilities outside of the larger communities, including those in Custer State Park (the exception being a few cabins at Blue Bell Lodge) are seasonal and usually closed in the winter. In addition, a number of roads in the Black Hills are closed in the winter because of snow.

In spite of these factors, a winter trip to the Black Hills is still worth considering to experience incredible solitude, good fishing or perhaps simply to witness the way winter transforms the mountains. If you are planning a winter fishing trip to the Black Hills, weather forecasts can be obtained via the National Oceanic and Atmospheric Administration's web page listed in the appendix. The site includes a handy little live web camera at Mt. Rushmore so you can survey current weather conditions for yourself.

LODGING AND CAMPING

There is ample lodging available throughout the Black Hills and in most communities adjacent to the area. Lodging ranges from the historic 1920s-era lodges of Custer State Park, to small "mom and pop" motel and cabin rentals, to national chain hotels located in Rapid City, Custer, Sturgis, Spearfish and elsewhere. Because the Black Hills are a well-known summer tourist destination, many of the cabins and small motels are seasonal. All of the Custer State Park lodges, except for a few cabins at Blue Bell Lodge, are also seasonal. Generally, the tourist season runs from around Memorial Day to October.

Lodging can be hard to come by during the peak summer tourist season in late summer and during the annual motorcycle rally in Sturgis each August.

Camping is permitted throughout the Black Hills National Forest except in certain developed areas around some of the lakes and along the right of way or at the trailheads of certain trails. Camping is also restricted in Custer State Park to designated camping areas. Open fires are not permitted in the Black Hills except in developed campgrounds or picnic areas.

There are also federal, state and private campgrounds throughout the Black Hills. The majority of the federal campgrounds have running water and primitive toilets but lack showers. Most developed state campgrounds have running water, primitive and flush toilets and showers. There are also federal and state campgrounds suited for large trailers and some take reservations for campsites. Private campgrounds vary as to the facilities that are available although most have running water and, at the very least, primitive toilets.

In the index, I have listed some, but by no means all, of the lodges and campgrounds located near or adjacent to the listed trout-fishing spots. The South Dakota Department of

Tourism publishes a guide to private, state and federal campgrounds in the Black Hills. The guide is available free-of-charge and can be obtained by calling the telephone number listed in the appendix. For additional lodging or camping locations consult travel guides or the applicable state and federal agencies listed in the appendix.

GETTING THERE

The Black Hills are located on the western edge of South Dakota and extend into northeastern Wyoming. U.S. Interstate 90 runs roughly northwest-southeast along the eastern edge of the Black Hills and then turns west, skirting its northern edge. Rapid City, the eastern gateway to the Black Hills, is 1,698 miles from New York City, 896 miles from Chicago, and 565 miles from Minneapolis. Spearfish, which is located on the northern tip of the Black Hills, is 1,130 miles from Seattle, Washington, and 325 miles from Billings, Montana. Custer, which lies within the southern Black Hills, is 359 miles from Denver.

Rapid City is served daily by a number of commercial airlines. Other than Rapid City, the nearest commercial airports to the Black Hills are in Sioux Falls, South Dakota, approximately 350 miles east of Rapid City, and Billings, Montana, which is 325 miles northwest.

WHEN TO GO

A year-round trout season, combined with winters milder than the surrounding region, make trout fishing in the Black Hills possible any time of the year. If you are planning a trout-fishing trip, there are a couple of factors to consider no matter what time of year you are going. The first is the tourist season. The Black Hills are a definite tourist attraction—with Mount Rushmore attracting roughly two million visitors each year. While you can generally find your own piece of water to fish in the Black Hills, even during the tourist season, federal and state campgrounds are often filled, as are many motels, and the main highways are busy. If you are planning a fishing trip during the tourist season, the height of which runs from Memorial Day to Labor Day—make sure you plan ahead and make lodging reservations.

Another factor to keep in mind is weather. If you are planning a winter fishing trip, call ahead or check the weather forecasts via the Internet to make sure that the weather won't make fishing impossible. In spring, heavy snowmelt can affect the quality of trout fishing, as can rain during the early summer months. For an up-to-the-minute report on stream conditions, log onto the web page of the Office of the United States Geological Survey (USGS) prior to your departure. This site lists flow rates for certain streams in the Black Hills. You can also make a call to officials with the South Dakota Game, Fish and Parks or Wyoming Game and Fish Department for more information. These websites and phone numbers are listed in the appendix.

While I like to visit and fish the Black Hills any time I can, my favorite time is September. By then, the weather has cooled down, there is less tourist traffic and the spectacular fall colors paint the hills everything but black. It's also a good time to see wildlife.

Part 2

Fishing The Black Hills

Wyoming's beautiful Sand Creek.

FISHING IN THE BLACK HILLS

FISHING REGULATIONS

To fish for trout in the Black Hills of South Dakota or Wyoming, you are required to purchase a fishing license from the state in which you plan to fish. These can be found at most fishing shops or sporting goods stores. Annual and daily fishing licenses are available to residents and non-residents.

South Dakota also offers annual family licenses and three-day licenses for non-residents. The non-resident annual family license allows the non-resident and his or her spouse and children under 16 to fish on a single license. However, the combined catch of all of the family members fishing with a family license may not exceed one daily possession limit.

Wyoming offers a cumulative daily license, allowing anglers to buy a license for the exact number of days they plan to fish. Anglers simply pay a set fee for each day of the license, up to ten days.

The fishing season for trout in the Black Hills of South Dakota and Wyoming runs year round, from January 1 to December 31. Special fishing regulations—including size and creel limits—exist throughout the region and are usually specified within both states' fishing regulation handbooks. The use of baitfish on Black Hills streams and in most of the lakes—with the exception of Sheridan and Stockade Lakes and Lake Pactola—is prohibited. In addition, many streams have individual special regulations in effect, ranging from the catch and release of certain types of trout and the required use of artificial lures and flies, to size limits for trout. For these and other regulations, consult the annual South Dakota or Wyoming fishing handbook.

ACCESSING TROUT WATERS

One of the things that make trout fishing in the Black Hills so unique and enjoyable is that the vast majority of its trout waters lie within federal or state lands. That means easy and generally unrestricted fishing access to creeks and lakes located within the 1.2-million-acre Black Hills National Forest and the 73,000 acre Custer State Park. Primary and secondary Forest Service and State Park roads allow good access to these streams and lakes including some that are fairly isolated. National Forest and South Dakota landholdings are usually well marked, making travel into these areas relatively easy. In addition, the State of Wyoming has negotiated easements on sections of Sand Creek to increase opportunities for public access.

When accessing trout waters on federal and state lands, there are a few guidelines that must be followed. If you are driving a motorized vehicle, you must stay on designated Forest Service or State Park Roads. Follow the regulations posted on all informational signs. Gates or other devices restricting motorized vehicles must not be crossed. It is also critical that you limit your impact on the streams, lakes and surrounding environment by staying on designated or obvious trails while hiking along a creek or lake. Finally, don't disturb wildlife, and pack out all garbage including leaders and spent fishing line.

Within the Black Hills there are also private landholdings, many of which are located along trout creeks. Generally, South Dakota law states that, with very few exceptions, "no person may fish on any private land not his own or in his possession without permission from the owner or lessee of such land." Persons found violating this law are subject to a misdemeanor and penalties. Under Wyoming water law, the landowner adjacent to a stream owns the streambed, meaning that you are trespassing even if you are standing in the middle of the stream.

To help you identify public and private landholdings, the United States Forest Service has produced a large color-coded map showing the boundaries of public and private lands in the Black Hills. The map can be purchased at most outdoor and fishing shops.

The vast majority of fishing locations listed in this book are on state and federal lands, making access questions irrelevant. There is so much good trout water lying within public lands that you don't need to cross private lands. However, if you just happen to see the biggest trout you have ever seen leap out of a section of creek surrounded by private land, and your trip to the Black Hills would be incomplete without throwing a fly in its direction, respect the rights of property owners by asking permission before crossing the private property.

EQUIPMENT

The Black Hills fisheries are made up of small spring-fed streams and manmade lakes, many of which are not more than a couple of acres in size. Some of the smaller brook trout streams are small enough to jump across. And while there are larger streams, like Rapid Creek and Spearfish Creek, even those are small by Montana, Wyoming or Colorado standards. While you can use equipment designed for larger bodies of water, if you're going to fish the Black Hills, it's a good idea to bring smaller, lighter rods and tackle if you have them. Otherwise, while you may be able to get the job done, your fishing won't be as successful or as enjoyable.

Overall, fly rods in the 7½-foot to 8½-foot, 4- to 5-weight range are about ideal for fishing in the Black Hills. I generally use a 7½-foot, 5-weight or an 8-foot, 4-weight fly rod on all the streams and most lakes. When I am fishing the bays or tailwaters of larger lakes like Pactola, Deerfield, Sylvan and others, I'll occasionally use a slightly longer rod.

The same rule applies for spin-casting equipment. Smaller, lighter rods with lighter line will be more effective for fishing Black Hills streams and lakes than the rod you use for catching large bass or walleyes. However, personal preference is a critical factor here and if you have a rod and reel you feel comfortable with that doesn't fall within these ranges, feel free to use it rather than rushing out and buying new equipment.

The second critical piece of equipment for successfully fly fishing Black Hills streams is your leader. If there is a rule of thumb when it comes to the use of leaders in the Black Hills, it is the longer the better. The leaders I use tend to be a minimum of 12 feet long. I also use long tippets in the 6X to 7X category. When fishing small crystal clear brook trout creeks like upper Castle Creek, Elk Creek or Little Spearfish Creek, I'll use 8X tippets.

Light also applies to wading gear. Because of the small, shallow nature of many streams, you can get by using hip waders or even less in summer. I often simply wear my wading boots, wading socks and shorts. Using lighter wading equipment will also make your fishing experience more enjoyable. While many streams and lakes are located at higher altitudes, it can still be very hot and the sun intense on summer days. I have seen a number of fishermen clad in neoprene waders climbing out of canyons on hot summer days red-faced and wheezing.

There are a few exceptions to these Black Hills wader

"rules." The first is winter. Those same heavy neoprene waders can prove to be quite comfortable on cold, snowy days. The second is high water due to spring thaws or heavy rains. In these cases, the small streams—especially those that flow from reservoirs—fill quickly with water and can become dangerously fast, wide and deep. When that happens, it's a good idea not to wade at all.

Float tubes and kick boats are very effective for fishing Black Hills lakes. These devices, available from a number of manufacturers and in a variety of models, will give you access to good locations on many of the smaller lakes. These lakes are too small for motorized craft but large enough in many cases to put fish out of reach.

Finally, it's a good idea to bring along some form of rain gear for a fishing trip to the Black Hills. Thunderstorms and rain are frequent occurrences, especially in the months of May and June when it can rain almost daily, if only briefly. The rain gear will make fishing more comfortable on rainy days when lightning isn't present.

Tips on Fishing Black Hills Creeks

If there is one word to consider when trout fishing the creeks of the Black Hills, that word is "stealth." If you want to understand what I mean, get out of your car or truck and walk normally over to the bank of one of the small creeks in the Black Hills. As you approach, watch the water closely and you'll see fish scattering up and downstream as you get near the creek. And it's likely many more scattered before you even got close enough to the creek to have been able to see the bottom.

Stealth. The majority of Black Hills creeks are small and shallow and, in periods of little or no rain, crystal clear. Some of the good brook trout streams, particularly those in the higher elevations, are so small that you can literally step across them. These factors, combined with a trout's natural wariness and fear of predators, require you to approach streams carefully and fish in a way that reduces the likelihood that a trout's fear and survival mechanisms will be triggered. Doing so will also help to increase the probability that you will catch fish.

To understand the importance of this, consider how a trout functions. A trout not only has the ability to look forward as it swims through the water; the position of its eyes also allows it to look outward and upward. The multiple functions of a trout's eyes suit it ideally for searching for food both in the water and on the surface. The ability to see an insect on the surface of the water also allows the trout to see beyond the surface and outward to the bank of a creek, if that creek is narrow enough. In addition, trout have the ability to detect vibrations, like someone or something walking through the water, thanks to a minute string of sense organs on the side of its body, called the "lateral line." A trout, while an extremely effective predator of insects and other aquatic life, knows that it is also the hunted. Man, raccoons, herons, ospreys and others are all threats to a trout's survival and the trout uses its unique vision and sensing ability to attempt to stay alive.

A trout lives, breathes and eats on a relatively small section of stream. It knows, or senses, when something is askew with that environment. The vibration of footsteps approaching the stream, silt kicked up by someone stepping across or standing in a stream, rocks being ground into the streambed by someone's wading boots, a line repeatedly splashed across the surface of the water, a hooked trout racing up and down a section of stream. All of these actions quickly tell the trout that something has changed in its environment and that change is not natural. A trout's survival mechanism then takes over and it quickly moves away from those dangers, interrupting its natural feeding pattern to stay alive.

For a stealthy approach to fishing Black Hills trout streams, consider the follow suggestions:

Dress to blend in with your environment. Before you even venture out to a stream to go trout fishing, plan your clothing carefully. Wear clothes, especially shirts and hats that blend into the environment or at the very least, clothes that don't make you stand out. Give yourself the "once over," checking for anything that will draw the attention of a trout like that nifty watch with the bright, shiny chrome band that reflects just about as much light as a mirror.

Survey the Creek. When you pull up near a stream and start to get your gear on and your equipment ready, take the time to survey the section of creek you are about to fish—if you can see it. Ask yourself: What's the best approach to the creek that will reduce the likelihood that the trout's fear mechanism will kick in? Am I going to fish upstream or downstream? Are there natural structures such as rocks, boulders or trees that I can use to help camouflage me from the trout? As you approach the creek, continue your survey, correcting your approach and fishing plans as necessary. How can I best cast to the trout I just saw rise? Will fishing for that trout affect fishing on the rest of this creek? Where are the pools, ledges, bank undercuts and other fish-holding structures? Answering these questions before you are streamside will reduce the likelihood of "spooked" trout and increase your chance of catching fish.

Approach carefully. Once you've decided where you are going to fish on the creek, approach carefully. Consider the fact that trout are constantly looking at the surface of the water and beyond. Keep your body, head and fishing rod below the trout's line of sight. Crawl on your hands and knees if necessary and use those structures you spotted in your survey to help camouflage your approach.

Let things calm down a bit. Once you reach the section of creek you are going to fish, pause for a few seconds. This will get you ready for your first cast and help to calm any of the trout's fears you may have kicked up on your approach.

Make your first cast count. Figure out where your first cast is going and for what purpose. If you are pursuing a rising trout, how can you best put that fly into the trout's feeding zone? If you are fly fishing, what is the best way to cast to avoid snags and hang-ups?

Move on or take a break when you put fish down. Catching a fish or two in a pool or particular section of creek is a sure way to trigger a trout's fear. When that happens, take a break for awhile or fish another section of the creek. Once the trout's environment has returned to what it considers safe, you can return to the section to fish again.

Don't wade if you don't have to. For some reason, many people who trout fish think wading is an integral past of the sport, no matter the size of the water. The sport isn't about wading, it's about catching fish (and enjoying nature while you're doing that). Wading is necessary when you are fishing a large river or stream, when you need to make a stream crossing or if it must be done in order to position yourself to catch a trout. Don't wade if you don't have to. Wading in clear shallow water is a good way to disrupt a trout's natural environment and quickly put it down.

TIPS ON FISHING BLACK HILLS LAKES

All of the lakes in the Black Hills are man-made and were created by damming small creeks and springs. The Works Progress Administration (WPA) and the Civilian Conservation Corps (CCC)—created to provide jobs and opportunities to Americans struggling to survive the Great Depression—constructed a number of the dams at the smaller lakes during the 1930s. In total, there were 29 CCC camps throughout the Black Hills whose workers, in addition to dam building, built bridges, trails, cabins and ranger stations.

Because most Black Hills lakes were created by damming small canyons, it's important to use caution, particularly when wading. In a matter of a just a few steps, a lake's bottom can quickly drop off, submerging an unsuspecting wader. If you are planning to do any wading, it's important to read and understand a lake's structure prior to fishing. Many of the marinas, stores and campgrounds have detailed lake elevation maps which are worth taking a look at, not only for the sake of safety, but also to improve the chance that you'll catch fish. These same drop-offs, or ledges, can be prime locations for trout.

Unlike streams with constantly moving water, lakes present a challenge, particularly to those fishing with a dry fly. Most aquatic insects need moving water to hatch. In addition, artificial flies don't move on still water and thus can be difficult to use in attracting fish.

If you are going to fish with a dry fly, there are a number of ways to remedy these challenges. One way is to find where there is moving water on the lake you are fishing. While it may not look like it at first glance, almost every lake will have some current or moving water. Because the majority of lakes were created by damming small creeks, the first location to find moving water is where the creek enters or leaves the lake. A lake's inlet, where the creek enters the lake, is often a prime feeding area for trout, which take advantage of the food and oxygen a creek carries downstream with it. A lake's outlet or spillway, particularly in higher water, also provides moving water and is a place to find feeding trout. Springs, which bring with them cold, oxygen-bearing water, are yet another place for moving water and feeding trout. Even small bays can be a source for moving water due to the lake pushing into and off of the shore.

If moving water is difficult to find, or if weather conditions make a lake's surface look like glass, moving or twitching the fly can be very effective. In this case, simply cast your fly onto the water and let it set for a few seconds until it is still. Then, using the tip of the rod, twitch the fly or lift it slightly off of the water, letting it set down again. This will help attract feeding trout and distinguish your fly from the twigs and dead insects that are constantly floating on the surface of the water. This is also very effective when using artificial grasshoppers, ants and other terrestrials.

Using the rod tip to move a fly on a lake's surface is a particularly effective technique for trout that are cruising around the lake looking for food. Unlike a stream—where a trout will often hold in a particular feeding location and wait for the current to deliver food—trout in lakes, particularly lakes with little current, often cruise around looking for insects on the surface, sipping, slashing, and dimpling the water along the way. When you see a cruising trout, watch its movement for a few moments and then attempt to anticipate the direction it is feeding and how it is feeding. Cast in front of it and let the fly lie still for a few seconds and then move it slightly. If the trout appears elsewhere, cast again.

Early morning and evening hours are good times for fishing Black Hills lakes with a dry fly, particularly from shore. If the conditions are right, trout are often actively feeding on a variety of hatching insects. Good spots to fish during these hours are locations that have moving water and, in particular, in a lake's bays and shallows.

If no trout appear to be rising, switch to subsurface flies, like streamers, nymphs or wet flies, and work the steep drop-offs and ledges. Use a weighted line and cast the fly along the edge of the drop-off, let it settle to the appropriate depth, then retrieve it with a quick stripping motion. Drift a subsurface fly through the inlet as well. Ledges and inlet streams are ideal locations for using spinning lures, as well.

Another place to look for trout, particularly in larger lakes, is in the stilling basin. While technically not part of a lake—a stilling basin is located below a dam—these stilling basins were constructed as a part of a reservoir to help control the outflow of water and silt from the lake. As a result. they tend to have constantly moving water. Lake Pactola and Deerfield Lake both have stilling basins that hold trout of decent size and number.

Black Hills lakes are ideal for fishing from float tubes and kick boats. Both are portable, easy to handle, and give you the ability to get to where the trout are. Float tubes and kick boats are particularly handy for fishing Lake Pactola's stilling basin, as well as lakes that are only few acres in size—tiny, yet large enough to make casting to certain locations on the lake difficult if not impossible without one.

USING THE TRAILS

The Black Hills have hundred of miles of trails—600 miles in the Black Hills National Forest alone—many of which allow for good access to trout fishing. In addition to hiking, some of the trails also permit horseback riding, cross-country skiing and mountain biking. A number of these trails were laid on old railroad grades, which threaded their way along the canyons and creeks. South Dakota's 114-mile Mickelson trail—named for the state's former governor who died in an airplane crash while in office—and the 111-mile Centennial Trail are just two of the many trails offering prime access to creeks and lakes.

These and other trails offer unique opportunities to hike and fish, or to fish via mountain bike, a combination sport becoming more popular. Day-long or even multi-day trout fishing hikes can be planned to take advantage of the network of trails in the Black Hills. Several of the good trout creeks can be reached by trail, including sections of both lower and upper Rapid Creek, French Creek, Grace Coolidge Creek, Little Elk Creek, Beaver Creek in Wyoming and sections of Spring Creek, Little Spearfish Creek and Slate Creek as well as numerous lakes.

If you are interested in a fishing trip via the Black Hills trail system, do some advance planning. Read the regulations and trail information carefully, and make sure, for example, that if you are planning a mountain biking trip, the trail you are interested in taking allows mountain bikes—wilderness areas do not. The regulations also include pertinent information regarding camping, water access and campfires. Above all, make sure your trip is planned in such a way as to minimize your impact on the environment.

You can obtain trail maps and trail information by contacting the United States Forest Service Black Hills office or the Black Hills Trails office. Addresses and telephone numbers are listed in the back of the book.

CATCH AND RELEASE

To paraphrase the legendary Lee Wulff, trout are too valuable to only catch once. While most fishermen have, at one time or another, kept a trout for breakfast or dinner, the practice of catch-and-release is becoming an important tool in preserving the limited numbers of wild trout in the Hills. Because the Black Hills are visited by roughly two million tourists each year, many bearing fishing rods, it's critical that catch-and-release be practiced, especially on streams where there are wild trout. Catch-and-release will help assure these fish will continue to flourish, allowing future generations to experience the beauty of wild trout.

With that said, proper catch-and-release requires more

than just throwing the fish back. What you do between the time you hook the fish and release it is key to its survival. Use artificial lures whenever possible because their use usually results in the trout being hooked in the lip. Barbless or crimped hooks also reduce the damage that can result from removing a hook. If a hook can't be removed for any reason, simply and quickly clip the line.

Play the fish for as short a time as possible, handle it as little as possible, and keep it in the water while removing the hook. Turning a trout upside down while you remove a hook will very often keep the fish from struggling, reducing the risk of further harming the fish. If it is necessary to touch the fish, and it often is, wet your hands first and then handle it gently. If a trout is exhausted, carefully hold it in a swimming position in the water and gently move it back and forth prior to releasing it. The motion will push oxygen-bearing water through the trout's gills and help revive it. Continue the motion until it swims away on its own.

SEVERE WEATHER

Some of the fiercest thunderstorms I have ever experienced have been in the Black Hills. The high altitude and the tendency of the mountains to stir up storms rumbling across the plains to the west, produce spectacular displays of lightening and thunder, as well as hail and high winds. These storms often come up quickly, seemingly out of nowhere.

Once when I was fishing Rapid Creek below Lake Pactola on a cloudy, muggy early summer day, the western sky turned black and green. I fished a while longer with a watchful eye to this front, which was obviously moving into the Black Hills. It arrived faster than I'd estimated. Suddenly the wind came up and the temperature dropped at least 15°F in minutes. Knowing from experience what was coming, I pulled my fly off the water and began to run the mile to my truck. By the time I got there, the sky had filled with lightning and the wind was literally rocking the truck. A few minutes later torrents of rain poured down, changing quickly to marble-size hail. The rain and hail were so intense it was impossible to drive, so I rode out the worst of the storm in the relative safety of my truck.

Experienced trout fishermen will tell you that some of the best fishing can occur just prior to a storm, and even in the rain as the storm front passes through. However, it's important to temper the desire for good fishing with good sense, especially in the Black Hills where in the month of June, thunderstorms form almost every afternoon. Take the time to check the local weather forecasts prior to going fishing and if severe storms are forecast, accept that as fact and plan accordingly. Take a weather radio with you if you can. Always keep a watchful eye to the sky and measure your distance to shelter carefully. If you hear the distant rumble of thunder, it's a good idea to move quickly to your car or shelter and take steps to protect yourself. Remember that lightning can strike miles from its parent cloud.

If caught in a lightning storm, the National Oceanic and Atmospheric Administration recommends taking a few common-sense steps. Don't linger on hilltops or high ground. Get away from open water and metal objects like fences; even a graphite rod is a dangerous conductor. If you are in a group, spread out. If you feel your hair stand on end, conditions are right for being struck. Crouch down, put your hands on your knees, and don't lie flat on the ground.

If there is one rule of Black Hills trout fishing that should never be broken, it is to respect the weather. If severe weather is threatening, take the threat seriously. There will always be another day to fish.

RATTLESNAKES

Yes, there are rattlesnakes (prairie rattlers) throughout the Black Hills, especially in its outer edges and mountain meadows. I became well aware of this fact one day when I was showing a friend the beautiful view of the northern Black Hills from the porch of my home near Spearfish. As I was pointing at a ridgetop that was rumored to have been the location of eagle-trapping pits used by the Lakota or Cheyenne, my friend said, "Is that a snake?" "Where?" I responded, scanning the yard. "Below you," he said. I looked down and lying a couple of feet away from my bare feet was a two-foot rattlesnake, stretched out on my porch, sunning itself.

If you do encounter a rattlesnake while fishing (though chances are you won't), you will likely hear it before you see it. The telltale rattling or buzzing of its rattles should serve as a warning to move on your way. They rattle because they aren't any more interested in an encounter with you than you are with them. The majority of strikes occur when you put your hand somewhere that you can't see, sit down without looking or when you don't look where you are walking. If you surprise a rattlesnake, it will strike to defend itself.

If you are, by off chance, struck by a rattlesnake, seek medical attention as soon as possible. Though a strike is a nasty situation to experience, due to the slow-acting nature of rattlesnake venom, most snake-bite victims survive, as long as they get prompt medical help.

USING THIS GUIDE

While most Black Hills streams have trout in varying numbers, at least in their headwaters, the following guide lists those streams and lakes with significant populations of trout, and where access is not restricted due to limited or restricted access, or private-property concerns. Lakes where the stocking of trout no longer occurs also were not included in the guide.

This guide divides the Black Hills into three regions and provides directions and maps to streams and lakes from

Spearfish, Rapid City or Custer, depending on the region. Where it made sense to do so, alternate directions are also provided. If you are driving to one of the listed streams or lakes from a different region or community, consult the official South Dakota or Wyoming highway maps, which include a section on the Black Hills, or the Forest Service's Black Hills National Forest map. The Forest Service map is available at Forest Service offices and most camping and hiking stores in the Black Hills.

The DeLorme Mapping Co. has also just recently produced a South Dakota Atlas and Gazetteer, which includes Global Positioning System (GPS) coordinates and other useful information for anglers and hikers in the high country.

The mileage listed in the directions to the streams and lakes is accurate to within approximately $1/10$ of a mile. When directions refer to locations to pull off of the road, those locations vary from primitive parking lots to little more than a widening of the shoulder where you can pull your vehicle off the highway or road. It is important for safety's sake, particularly on heavily used roads and highways, to park your vehicle *completely* off the road.

INSECTS HATCHES AND FLY SELECTION

The hatch chart on the opposite page is intended simply to give you an idea of which insect hatches you could encounter in the Black Hills. Hatches vary from stream to stream, and from year to year. Consult one of the local fly shops or sporting goods stores listed in the Appendix for a more accurate report on which hatches you're likely to find at the time you'll be in the Hills, and which flies to carry.

The Black Hills are home to some truly great flytiers, and each of the fly shops in the area carries several local patterns and variations on traditional patterns developed by these flytiers.

Species	Common Name or Imitation	Size	Jan.	Feb.	Mar.	April	May	June	July	Aug.	Sept.	Oct.	Nov.	Dec.
MAYFLIES														
Baetis	Blue-wing Olive, Tiny BWO	14-22	■	■								■		
Rhithrogena	Western Red Quill, et al	12-16					■	■						
Callibaetis	Speckled Spinner, Adams, et al	14-18					■	■	■	■	■			
Tricorythodes minutus	Trico	20-28							■	■	■			
Ephemerella spp	Pale Morning Dun, Pale Eve. Dun	16-22					■	■	■	■				
Pseudocloëon	Blue-wing Olive	20-28						■	■	■	■	■		
CADDISFLIES														
Brachycentrus spp	Grannom Caddis	14-16					■	■			■			
Hydropsyche spp	Spotted Sedge	14-16						■	■	■	■			
Hydroptilidae spp	Microcaddis	18-22					■	■	■	■	■	■		
Glossosomatidae	Tan Sedge	14-16					■	■	■	■				
Leptoceridae	Longhorn Sedge	14-18						■	■	■	■			
MIDGES	Tan, Gray, Olive, Yellow, Black	20-28	■	■	■	■	■	■	■	■	■	■	■	■
STONEFLIES														
Capnia	Little Black, Early Black Stone	14-18	■	■	■	■								
Isoperla spp	Little Yellow Stone	14-18						■	■	■				
Pterynarcys spp	Giant Black Stone	2-6					■	■						
TERRESTRIALS	Beetles, Ants / Hoppers	12-22 / 4-10							■	■	■	■		
DAMSELFLIES, DRAGONFLIES	Damsel nymphs, wooly buggers	4-10						■	■	■				

53

Part 3

The Trout Streams and Lakes of The Black Hills

A Spearfish Canyon pond.

THE NORTHERN BLACK HILLS

SPEARFISH CREEK • LITTLE SPEARFISH CREEK •
HANNA CREEK (EAST SPEARFISH CREEK) • BEAVER
CREEK (SOUTH DAKOTA) • ELK CREEK • MCNENNY
HATCHERY REGION: CROW CREEK, COXES LAKE,
MIRROR LAKE • SAND CREEK • BEAVER
CREEK (WYOMING) • IRON CREEK LAKE •
REAUSAW LAKE • STRAWBERRY HILL POND

The Black Hills are roughly divided into three regions: The Northern, Central and Southern Hills. The first of these, the Northern Black Hills, covers an area stretching from Spearfish, South Dakota to the Bear Lodge Range in eastern Wyoming, south to Wyoming's Sand Creek, and east to the little settlement of Nemo, South Dakota. Most of the streams and lakes in this section lie within South Dakota's Lawrence County.

The best-known, and most-visited, natural feature of this region is Spearfish Canyon. The canyon has much to offer: a healthy population of wild rainbow trout, a spectacular array of fall colors from a thick growth of aspen in the area, mountain goats peering over the canyon's rim, towering limestone and shale walls, waterfalls. It's little wonder why Spearfish Canyon is one of the most popular destinations in the Black Hills—especially for South Dakotans.

Spearfish Canyon, and the area around it, is characteristic of the plateau region of the Black Hills, with its deep limestone canyons and shales and slates. The Canyon, which is older than the Grand Canyon, was created over millions of years as the drainage from the area that became Spearfish Creek slowly eroded the soft limestone.

Spearfish Creek, which snakes its way through Spearfish Canyon, is the dominant body of water in the northern Black Hills. The creek rises near the Wyoming border, flowing northeasterly until it reaches Cheyenne Crossing—where the old Deadwood-to-Cheyenne stagecoach route crossed the creek. From Cheyenne Crossing, the creek flows northward, entering Spearfish Canyon. The creek flows through the Canyon for a little over eighteen miles until it flows out of the Black Hills and through the community of Spearfish. As it wanders through Spearfish Canyon, it picks up Hanna Creek and Little Spearfish Creek, two popular trout streams in the northern Black Hills. Squaw Creek also joins Spearfish Creek in the Canyon as does Iron Creek. Squaw Creek serves as a nursery of sorts for wild rainbow trout and is home to a unique geological feature known as the Devil's Bathtubs—a series of deep cascading pools created by water erosion.

West of Spearfish Creek, no more than a couple of miles into Wyoming, lies Sand Creek. Winding its way through a dramatic, rough-hewn canyon of limestone and sandstone, Sand Creek is fed by a spring that produces an abundance of fast-flowing water with a year-round average temperature of 56°F. In addition to being a significant fishery, the creek is important historically to Wyoming because it is the location of "Ranch A," the 1930s retreat of the Annenburg family.

To the southwest of Sand Creek lies Sundance, Wyoming, named after the sacred Lakota sun dance which, according to legend, took place where the community is now located. To the north of Sundance is the craggy Bear Lodge Range, the western extent of the Black Hills.

The rest of the northern Black Hills are also full of history. Bear Butte, the sacred mountain of the Lakota and Cheyenne, is located a few miles east of Sturgis. There is a hiking trail to the mountain's summit and its trees are covered with prayer cloths and tobacco offerings. Many of the trees have small stones placed within the branches as offerings. In some trees, the branches have grown around the stones, evidence of how long the tradition has been practiced. At the base of Bear Butte it is not uncommon to see small domed sweat lodges used by Indians purifying themselves in preparation for a vision quest. Sturgis, of course, has its own history. Home of the annual Sturgis motorcycle rally, one week every summer it fills with the rumble of tens of thousands of motorcycles.

A short drive to the west of Sturgis is Deadwood. In the 1800s, Deadwood personified the rough-and-tumble town of the Wild West. The former haunt of Calamity Jane, Buffalo Bill, Potato Creek Johnny, and Deadwood Dick, to name just a few, it is also where Wild Bill Hickok met his death with a bullet while playing poker in a saloon. The hand he held—black aces and eights—became immortalized as the "dead man's hand."

In November of 1989, South Dakota legalized gambling in Deadwood. With revenue gained from gambling, Deadwood has restored its commercial district and cobblestone streets in an effort to harken back once again to the era of the late 1800s.

The town of Spearfish, of course, takes its name from the creek that flows through town. It is the largest community in the northern Black Hills. It is also home to the restored D.C. Booth Fish Hatchery, the hatchery that played a major role in trout propagation in the Black Hills and in Yellowstone Park during the early 1900s. D.C. Booth is on the National Register of Historic Places and now serves as a fisheries museum.

The trout fishing in the northern Black Hills is outstanding. Spearfish Creek and its tributaries hold plentiful populations of wild rainbow, brown and brook trout. Sand Creek, one of the most significant brown trout fisheries in the United States, is also home to rainbow, brook and cutthroat trout. There are also lakes and ponds high in the mountains filled with hatchery-stocked rainbow trout. On the northern edge of the Black Hills, as the mountains begin to taper into grasslands and red buttes, is the McNenny Hatchery region. The region contains Crow Creek, one of the most productive wild brown trout creeks in western South Dakota, as well as deep spring-fed lakes, no more than a few acres in size, perfect for an afternoon of fishing from a float tube or kick boat.

The scenery around Mirror Lake, near the McNenny Hatchery on the northern edge of the Black Hills, is a marked contrast to the rest of the Black Hills region.

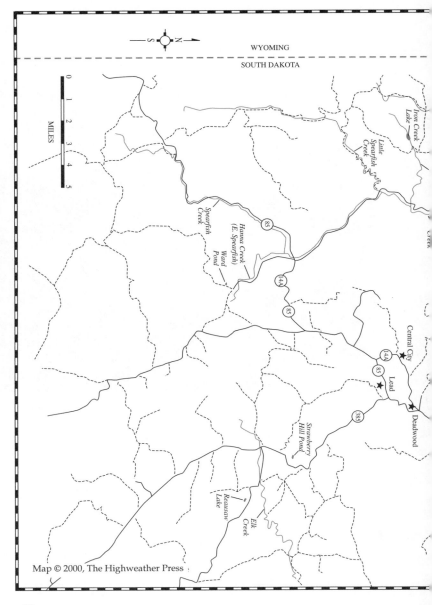

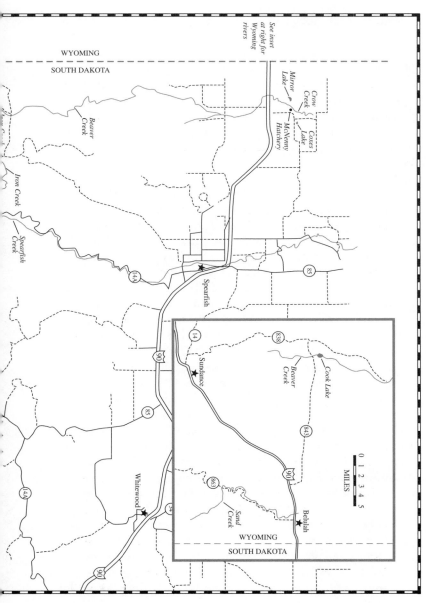

SPEARFISH CREEK

Arguably the most popular creek in the Northern Black Hills, Spearfish Creek is deserving of its popularity—for its scenery and its fishing. There are two legends of how Spearfish Creek got its name. One says the creek was a place where Indians in the area would commonly spear for fish. The second is that early gold explorers commented on what a good spot the creek would be for spearing fish. Whichever is true, Spearfish Creek has a long history of fish and fishing.

Prior to the introduction of trout into the Black Hills, the fish most commonly found and caught in the creek were probably chubs or suckers. However, once trout were introduced—Spearfish Creek was one of the locations for the early stocking experiments—trout fishing soon became a synonym for both the creek and the canyon.

In the late 1800s, a railroad line from Spearfish to Deadwood was built in the canyon, allowing tourists, sightseers and fishermen to easily visit their favorite spots. Family fishing outings on Spearfish Creek via railroad were common in the early 20th century. Although the rail line is long gone, the creek remains a popular fishery with healthy populations of wild brown, rainbow and brook trout.

Trout fishing on Spearfish Creek starts in the town of Spearfish. Much of the creek has been improved, including the section that winds through the town. While fishing is good throughout the community, a popular location is the city park. To get there, take Main Street south through downtown Spearfish and turn right on Grant Street. Stay on Grant Street for a few blocks until you reach Canyon Street where you will turn left. On Canyon Street you will see the city park on your right and you will eventually come to a parking area on your right with an archway leading into it. Park there and you can fish the creek upstream or down. Within the park, the creek is wheelchair accessible. A few hundred feet farther down Canyon Street is the parking lot for the historic D.C. Booth Hatchery, which is worth a visit.

The next stop on Spearfish Creek is in the Canyon itself. Follow Main Street south out of Spearfish. A few blocks out of downtown Spearfish, Main Street turns into County Boulevard. Stay on County Boulevard until you reach Highway 14A. Turn right onto Highway 14A driving past a golf course on your left. As you drive down Spearfish Canyon you'll begin to see the high limestone and shale walls for which the canyon is famous.

About 4 miles after turning onto Highway 14A you'll see an intake, or diversion, dam on your left. From here upstream into the Canyon, there is sufficient water in Spearfish Creek to support trout. (Water diversion dams intermittently rob this creek of its water—and trout. It is a situation you'll find throughout the West.) Park on the right side of the road and fish upstream from the dam. A little more than ½ mile beyond this first stop, there is another place on the right side of the road to park and fish.

About 5¾ miles from the Highway 14A turn-off, you'll pass on your left one of the two waterfalls in Spearfish Canyon. Known as Bridal Veil Falls, it has long been a tourist attraction in the Canyon. The flow of Bridal Veil Falls varies from a trickle to a torrent, depending on water conditions.

Approximately 7 miles from the Highway 14A turn-off, you will come to a special regulation catch-and-release-only zone, indicated by a large sign near the stream on the left side of the road. Starting here at a small dam, and running upstream for a little more than one mile to a small hydro-electric plant, Spearfish Creek sustains a population of wild rainbow trout, as well as browns. To help sustain the trout population, the state has made stream improvements on this section of creek. And the fast water along here makes fishing a challenge. At the beginning of the catch-and-release section you can park at the parking area on the left side of the road.

Approximately 7½ miles from the Highway 14A turn-off you will come to Squaw Creek, which flows into Spearfish Creek through a steep canyon on your left. A small marker on the left side of the road with the number 19, and a bridge crossing Spearfish Creek mark the spot. Squaw Creek is a significant feature of Spearfish Canyon for a number of reasons. In addition to containing a small population of brook trout, it is used as a spawning ground for wild rainbow trout and serves as a "nursery" for the fry. It is also home to the "Devil's Bathtub," a series of deep pools created by water erosion. On the upper reaches of Squaw Creek are the tumble-down remnants of an abandoned gold mine. Devil's Bathtub is approximately one mile up Squaw Creek from its confluence with Spearfish Creek and the mine is roughly 1½ miles upstream. You can fish up or downstream from the bridge that crosses Spearfish Creek at this location or, if you want to take a break from fishing, hike up Squaw Creek.

Further upstream on Spearfish Creek, on the left side of Highway 14A, you will pass two huge boulders that are lying in the stream—a popular photo spot for tourists. Beyond that, approximately 10½ miles from the Highway 14A turn-off, you will come to the Long Valley picnic area on your left. This is another good location to park and fish upstream. At approximately 11 miles, Iron Creek flows into Spearfish Creek from the west. There is a parking area on the right side of the road adjacent to the creek and a trail that runs upstream. The lower section of Iron Creek, while difficult to fish because of streamside growth, contains a decent population of brown trout. Fishing is also good at the confluence of Spearfish and Iron Creek.

A little over 12 miles after turning onto Highway 14A, you will come to a sign for a curve in the road. Watch closely because immediately after that sign there is a parking area on the left shoulder of the road before the guard rail begins, marked by an old "no overnight camping" sign.

Park there and take the trail down to the creek and fish upstream, where you will encounter a series of riffles, pools and bends in the creek.

Approximately 13 miles up the canyon on Highway 14A you will reach Savoy. Now the site of a hotel and history center, Savoy was originally the location of a sawmill and, later, the Latchstring Inn—an inn that was known for its massive stone fireplaces and breakfasts of trout and blueberry pancakes. To the west of Savoy on Little Spearfish Creek is Spearfish Canyon's second waterfall—Roughlock Falls on Little Spearfish Creek.

South of Savoy, Spearfish Creek begins to narrow but the fishing is still excellent. To fish upstream from Savoy, continue driving south down the canyon on Highway 14A. The highway follows the creek and for the next few miles there are several popular places to park and fish.

At a little under four miles south of Savoy you will reach a sign for Elmore—a former stop for the train that ran through Spearfish Canyon. At Elmore, you will cross a bridge on Highway 14A and there will be a parking area on your right. Fishing upstream on this section, to Cheyenne Crossing, is excellent and one of my favorite spots to fish on Spearfish Creek. There are private cabins in this area and some of the land adjacent to the creek is privately owned, so it is important to respect private property rights on this stretch.

The next stop on Spearfish Creek is approximately 4½ miles south of Savoy on Highway 14A. You will see two spring-fed ponds on your right that lie between the highway and the creek. They are known as the Upper and Lower Yates ponds. Although small, the ponds are home to a large population of adult brown and brook trout, which is also the reason the ponds are currently special-regulation waters, with a catch-and-release-only policy. There is a parking area adjacent to the ponds. If you fish there, don't overlook fishing on the section of Spearfish Creek directly behind the ponds where fishing can also be excellent. (There are utility wires near the ponds so watch your casts, otherwise your fishing line and your fly or spinner will be added to the collection dangling from the wires.)

A few hundred feet south of the Yates ponds Spearfish Canyon officially ends at Cheyenne Crossing—the point where the Deadwood-to-Cheyenne stagecoach crossed Spearfish Creek. However, fishing on the creek does not end here. While it becomes increasingly narrow as you move upstream, there are still another 12 miles of creek until you reach the headwaters. And though the trout aren't as plentiful on this stretch as they are in some of the locations within the canyon, you still stand a good chance of finding decent numbers of brown and brook trout. One good spot is approximately ½ mile west of Cheyenne Crossing on Highway 85 where you can park on the left side of the road and fish the creek upstream or down.

Little Spearfish Creek

Little Spearfish Creek is a tributary to Spearfish Creek. It flows over Roughlock Falls, a popular tourist attraction in the northern Hills. The creek is small with a lot of streamside growth and overhangs that can make fishing difficult in certain locations, but there is also a healthy population of wild brown and brook trout. Little Spearfish Creek is a popular destination with fly anglers. It has a hike-in area that can be accessed via a trailhead.

There are several good spots on Little Spearfish Creek that are easy to access—and fairly easy to fish. To get to the first of these, drive south out of Spearfish on Main Street, which curves to the left and becomes Canyon Street. On the east edge of Spearfish, you'll reach the junction of Highway 14A. Turn right onto Highway 14A and drive south for approximately 13 miles until you reach Savoy. At Savoy, turn right onto Forest Service Road 222, following the signs for Roughlock Falls. Almost immediately, you will pass the parking area for the Spearfish Canyon Lodge on the left, and, immediately after that, you will come to another parking area on your left. Park in the second parking area and follow the hiking trail, which is on the southeast corner of the parking lot. The trail follows the creek. Stay on the trail until you have passed a small dam on the right. As you walk upstream, you will see a small meadow on your right where fishing is good. You can fish from there up to the base of the falls, using the hiking trail for easy access.

The next spot to fish on Little Spearfish Creek is further up the canyon. Get back onto Forest Service Road 222 and drive past Roughlock Falls, which was named for the practice of locking the wheels of a horse- or mule-drawn wagon to slow it down and make it easier to control on a steep downhill descent. Approximately 2¾ miles from the turn-off at Savoy, you'll pass a sign on the right marking where one of the final scenes from the movie *Dances with Wolves* was shot. Just beyond this point, you'll come to the Rod and Gun Campground, which is a little under 3 miles from Savoy. Several hundred feet upstream from the campground, the creek passes through a small meadow on the right side of the road, where the 1997 "America's Holiday Tree" was harvested. You can park at the campground and work your way up through the meadow.

Another good spot on Little Spearfish Creek is a hike-in location that is part of a popular network of trails in the area. To get there, drive past the Rod and Gun Campground on Forest Service Road 222 until you reach the Timon Campground, which is approximately 4½ miles from the turn-off at Savoy. Just as you pass the Timon Campground there's a parking area for a trailhead on the left. Park at the trailhead and access the Upper Little Spearfish Creek hiking trail, which runs perpendicular to the parking area, and walk up into the canyon. Little Spearfish Creek will be to your left. You can fish anywhere along the creek at this point or you can continue walking up the trail until you pass a large tan-and-red limestone cliff on your right. After the cliff, there will be a meadow on the left. The creek at this location and further upstream has good fishing.

HANNA CREEK (EAST SPEARFISH CREEK)

Though commonly referred to by everyone who knows it as Hanna Creek, this piece of water in the northern Black Hills is actually East Spearfish Creek. No matter what it is called, it is a sweet little trout stream, small but full of structure and wild brown and brook trout. Hanna Creek (we'll stick with what the locals call it) is a tributary of Spearfish Creek, flowing into it at Cheyenne Crossing.

To reach Hanna Creek from Spearfish, drive south on Main Street, which turns into County Boulevard. Stay on County Boulevard until you reach Highway 14A. Turn right onto Highway 14A, driving south for approximately 18¼ miles until you reach Cheyenne Crossing. When you reach Cheyenne Crossing and the junction of Highway's 14A and 85, turn right, going west on Highway 85 for a few hundred feet until you see a bridge that crosses Spearfish Creek. There you will see a sign for the Hanna Campground. Just before the bridge, turn left onto the road (Forest Service Road 196) toward the Hanna campground.

As you drive FS 196, the road runs parallel to Hanna Creek, crossing it several times. Continue for a little over a mile until you reach an area where you can park on the right shoulder of the road. The fishing here is good both upstream and downstream.

To get to the next location to park and fish on Hanna Creek, drive just a little under two miles from the Highway 85 turnoff. There you will cross a bridge where you will see parking areas on you left and right. Fishing is good upstream and downstream from this location as well. Further up the road, a little less than a ¼ mile away from this stop, is the Hanna Campground where you can also park and fish up or downstream.

The last stop on Hanna Creek is approximately 3½ miles from where you turned onto Forest Service Road 196 from Highway 85. You will pass a large brick building on your left and a little more than a ¼ mile past the building, you will come to Forest Service Road 209. Turn right onto FS 209 and a few hundred feet up the road you will come to Ward Pond. You can fish the pond, which is known to produce lots of brook trout as well as an occasional, decent-sized rainbow trout—holdovers from past stockings.

An alternate route to access Hanna Creek is to drive west of Deadwood/Lead on Highway 85 passing the turn-offs for Terry Peak and Deer Mountain ski resorts on your right. Highway 85 will descend a large hill and Cheyenne Crossing will be at the base of the hill. Follow the above directions once you have reached Cheyenne Crossing.

BEAVER CREEK

Beaver Creek is a small meandering creek high in the northern Black Hills, near the Wyoming border. It runs through an isolated mountain meadow west of Iron Creek Lake. The creek has been improved and holds a small population of wild brook trout, as well as wild and stocked browns. One of the unique aspects of Beaver Creek is that, because of its location, it is one of those Black Hills creeks with limited fishing pressure. The times I have fished there, I have never seen another person on the creek.

To get to Beaver Creek, follow the route to Iron Creek Lake (p. 81). Instead of turning left off of Forest Service Road 222 to Iron Creek Lake, stay on this road for approximately 1½ miles past the lake turnoff. At that point, you'll come to a couple of culverts where Beaver Creek flows under the road. Right after crossing the culverts, park on the left shoulder of the road. At this point you'll see a primitive road that runs upstream to the south. Follow this road on foot (it crosses private land) until you reach the Forest Service gate, which marks the start of public property. Climb the gate and start fishing upstream as soon as you are on Forest Service property.

ELK CREEK

Elk Creek is a small, spring-fed creek that winds its way through the northeastern Black Hills. The creek is known to hold a healthy population of brook trout—some of which can get quite large—and some brown trout. However, much of the creek is on private land making access difficult on most stretches.

A good section to fish is near the hamlet of Roubaix. Accessing the creek in this location requires a ¾-mile hike and the use of a United States Forest Service map to make sure that you don't stray onto private property. However, if you are attracted to the lure of Black Hills' brook trout, this section is worth the effort.

To get to this spot, drive east from Spearfish on Interstate 90 for approximately 5½ miles to the junction of Highway 85. Turn right onto Highway 85 driving through Deadwood to the junction of Highway 385. Turn left onto Highway 385, driving south for a little more than 7½ miles to Nemo Road. Turn left onto Nemo Road and drive east for approximately 1½ miles until you come to a sharp right curve. Just as you go into the curve there will be a United States Forest Service access point on the left, marked by signs and a section of asphalt leading off Nemo Road.

Turn into the access road and park, making sure you

don't block the entrance. Walk up the access road, which curves uphill to the right until you come to a gate. Go through the gate (make sure you close it behind you) and turn to your left, walking down hill until you reach the Forest Service property fence. Stay on Forest Service property and follow the fence east for roughly ¾ of a mile, past a powerline, past where the creek runs along the fence, and then onto an old roadbed. Follow the roadbed until it opens into a meadow and the creek turns south. Fish downstream from this point for roughly ¾ of a mile, until you come to a small piece of private property. Skirt the private property and continue fishing downstream for approximately a mile.

Note: There is not a trail to access this section of Elk Creek and there is lots of fallen timber, so it's a good idea to keep your fly rod in its case until you reach the public access section.

McNenny Hatchery Region

The area around the McNenny Hatchery west of Spearfish near the Wyoming border is a productive and fun area to fish. Encompassing several small lakes and a creek with wild brown trout, the area is home to some of the best fishing in the northern Black Hills. Moreover, the scenery around the lakes and creek is a marked contrast to the rest of the Black Hills. Here, the terrain is open grassland more typical of eastern Wyoming.

McNenny Hatchery was constructed in the 1950s as a replacement hatchery for the D.C. Booth Hatchery in Spearfish, which was suffering from declining water quality and quantity. There is a cluster of springs in the area around the hatchery, which provide a cold (52°F year-round) and dependable flow of water, creating conditions perfect for trout.

To access the fishing areas near McNenny Hatchery,

drive west from Spearfish on Interstate 90. The wide, sweeping valley to the north of the Interstate is characteristic of the red sandstone, siltstones and buttes of the foothills and the "racetrack." The Lakota, Cheyenne and other tribes used the valley as they moved back and forth from the Black Hills into the Powder River region of what is now northeastern Wyoming and southeastern Montana. Approximately 7 miles west of Spearfish on Interstate 90, you will reach South Dakota Exit 2. Exit here and turn right at the bottom of the ramp, following the signs to the McNenny Hatchery.

CROW CREEK

Crow Creek is a great place to fish. Unlike the rest of the Black Hills where the streams are surrounded by pines and rock outcroppings, much of Crow Creek winds through a nearly treeless valley to Redwater Creek. The creek is home to a naturally reproducing population of wild brown trout. Cutthroat, which are most likely escapees from when the hatchery raised the species in the early 1990s, can also occasionally be found in the creek. It is currently a special-regulation creek, requiring fishermen to release trout over 10 inches and to use artificial lures only. As of this writing, the special-regulation status of Crow Creek is under review by officials with the South Dakota Department of Game, Fish and Parks.

There are several places to access and fish Crow Creek. To get to these locations, follow the above directions to McNenny Hatchery. Turn into the entrance of the Hatchery. The road forks immediately; take the left fork and you'll come to a small bridge crossing Crow Creek. Immediately before the bridge, you can park on your right and fish downstream. To get to the second place to fish, take the first right after crossing the small bridge and park on the north side of the lake, which you will pass on your left. Crow

Creek is immediately to the east of the parking area on the north side of the lake.

My favorite area to fish on Crow Creek is north of the McNenny Hatchery. To get there, follow the above directions to the hatchery from Spearfish, but instead of turning left into the hatchery, stay on the road that curves to the right. Take the first left turn you come to and drive north a little over half a mile and you will see a gate on the left side of the road. You will also see Crow Creek in the valley to your left and a small bridge that crosses the creek. Park at the gate, hike down to the Creek and fish upstream or downstream from the bridge.

COXES LAKE

Some maps of the Black Hills don't show Coxes Lake (which is also known as "Cox" Lake). For that reason, and because it is not visible from the area around the McNenny Hatchery, it is often overlooked. It is, in itself, a wonder of nature. The lake, barely three acres in size, is actually a spring-fed sinkhole formed when a piece of the fragile Spearfish limestone formation collapsed due to erosion. Small dam impoundments, built during the 1950s, increased the surface area of the lake to its present size. What is most amazing about Coxes Lake is its depth. Recent measurements have found the lake to be nearly 90 feet deep. On a clear, calm day, the structure of the lake is evident, with its center looking like a dark blue-black hole.

Coxes Lake is stocked with hatchery rainbow trout and is known to hold some very large fish. It has a couple of fishing docks on its west side to make fishing the deeper areas from shore a little easier. One late afternoon when I was at the lake, I watched a fly-fisherman in a float tube catch and release a couple dozen trout in the 12- to 18-inch range in a very short period of time.

To get to Coxes Lake, follow the directions to McNenny Hatchery, driving past its entrance. You will come to a curve in the road after which you will take the first left you come to. Drive a little less than a quarter of a mile and you will come to a road on the right into a grassland area that is marked with several game production signs. Turn onto this road until you reach the lake. The fishing docks are located next to the parking area.

MIRROR LAKE

Mirror Lake ought to be called "Mirror Lakes," because it is actually two small lakes, each approximately three acres. Like Coxes Lake, Mirror Lake is made up of spring-fed sink-holes linked by a series of small dams and is home to a population of large, hatchery planted rainbow trout.

To get to Mirror Lake, follow the directions for McNenny Hatchery. When you come to the entrance for the hatchery, turn left. When the hatchery road forks, take the left fork. You will then cross a small bridge at which point the road forks again. If you take the right fork, you will end up at the east lake. The left fork takes you to the west lake which, like Coxes Lake, has small fishing docks. As of this writing, the west lake is a special-regulation lake, allowing only one fish over 16 inches to be kept.

SAND CREEK

Sand Creek is to the Black Hills of Wyoming what Spearfish, Rapid and French Creeks are to the Black Hills of South Dakota. It has an abundant and diverse population of wild, naturally reproducing trout, containing brown, rainbow, brook and cutthroat trout. It also has history, having been the location of "Ranch A", the western retreat of the

Annenburg family, famous East Coast financiers. The structures at the ranch were built in the 1930s, and later became the retreat for many prominent Wyoming citizens.

From 1963 to 1979, Ranch A was owned by the United States Fish and Wildlife Service and served as its genetic laboratory, due in large part to the spring located on Sand Creek which produces a constant source of 56°F water. In the 1980s, it became part of the federal hatchery system, serving in conjunction with the Spearfish hatchery as its Diet Development Center. It later became part of the Wyoming hatchery system. Today, Ranch A serves as a retreat center.

Sand Creek is the dominant fishing water within the Wyoming section of the Black Hills as it flows into and through the foothills. While the trout in Sand Creek are not large, they more than make up for it in number. Officials with the Wyoming Game and Fish Department estimate that Sand Creek has one of the largest per-mile brown trout populations in the United States. The presence of the spring at Ranch A, and the fact that Wyoming has a year-round season for trout, make fishing possible on Sand Creek any time of the year. That, coupled with prolific hatches and the creek's beautiful structure, make Sand Creek a fly angler's dream.

The canyon through which Sand Creek runs rivals the natural beauty of any other location in the Black Hills. The rim of the canyon is capped with limestone and sandstone, the colors of which seem to glow in the early morning or late evening light. The creek is lined with scrub oak and boxelder. The trees, along with the cool spring-fed water, make fishing on the creek comfortable even on 100-degree days. Like much of the rest of the Black Hills, wildlife is abundant in the area. Deer, wild turkey and elk are all common to the area.

Because of the importance of Sand Creek to Wyoming's fishery system, the state has gone to great lengths to make stream access possible through public fishing easements. It has also developed access roads and posted signs, further increasing the ease of fishing this great piece of water.

To fish Sand Creek, drive west of Spearfish on Interstate 90 for approximately 11 miles, crossing into Wyoming and exit at Beulah, Wyoming. Turn left at the top of the exit ramp onto Forest Service Road 863, following the signs for Ranch A.

Approximately ½ mile after exiting the interstate onto FS 863, you will come to the first public access area for Sand Creek on the right. There is a parking area on the bluff overlooking the creek. From this location, upstream for approximately three miles (in road miles), the stream is open to public fishing. An additional parking area is located another half mile up the road from the first stop.

Approximately two miles after exiting the interstate and driving onto FS 863, you will come to the first of a series of access roads for state campsites located along Sand Creek. Upstream from the second camping area, located approximately 2½ miles from the interstate, is a stretch of water viewed by many to be one of the best sections of the public easement water, due in part, to the creek's spectacular structure. This area is marked by a small warden's cabin that sits streamside.

Approximately ½ mile further down FS 863 from the last of the state camping areas, you will enter the property of the Sand Creek Country Club, which strenuously prohibits public fishing on its grounds. It's roughly a 1½-mile drive through the Country Club grounds after which you will enter Ranch A, marked by a stone archway on the right side of the road. Immediately after entering Ranch A, there is a parking area on the right side of the road.

Upstream from the north entrance of Ranch A is the favorite Sand Creek fishing spot of Dale Daniels, a well-known fly-fisherman from Sundance, Wyoming. Daniels has fished Sand Creek for over 20 years and has even been seen on this section of creek, fly rod in hand, on Christmas Day. The section of creek running through Ranch A has special regulations allowing the use of artificial lures and flies only.

Sand Creek winds through Ranch A, past the old hatchery buildings, below which are several good pools, and then past the main ranch house. The ranch house, with its imposing log porch supports, is considered one of the finest hand-hewn log buildings in the West. The house and associated buildings were completed in 1935 at a cost well in excess of $1 million—in depression-era dollars. The entire estate was once surrounded by a fence, and contained a kind of private zoo.

The last section to fish on Sand Creek is directly upstream from the ranch house on the south end of Ranch A. As you drive down the road you'll see a small impoundment on the creek on the left side of the road. You can pull over and park on the shoulder of the road and fish this section upstream until the creek dwindles down to a trickle. While the trout are not as abundant on this section as they are downstream, there is still a significant population and the fish seem larger.

Note: Rattlesnakes are common on Sand Creek and poison ivy is abundant, so be cautious where you walk.

BEAVER CREEK (WYOMING)

Beaver Creek is the dominant creek within the Bear Lodge Mountains, part of the westernmost sector of the Black Hills National Forest. The Bear Lodge Mountains lie directly north of Sundance, Wyoming. Sundance takes its name from the legend that the Lakota held their sacred sun dance at the present location of the community. The town, with a population of 1,100 people, sits within a natural basin, surrounded by mountains and ridges.

Beaver Creek flows into and out of Cook Lake, the only lake of any significant size in the Bear Lodge Mountains. The lake, which sits at 4,800 feet, features a picnic area, a campground with 34 campsites, and a hiking trail that follows a portion of the creek downstream. At one time, Cook Lake was a significant trout fishery, but the unauthorized introduction of sunfish and bullheads has caused the trout population to decline dramatically.

One of the best locations to fish the creek is below Cook Lake, where it is supplied with a steady source of water. The hiking trail follows the creek downstream from the dam through a canyon, providing easy access to a series of runs and pools that contain healthy populations of wild brown, brook and rainbow trout.

To access Beaver Creek below Cook Lake, drive west of Spearfish on Interstate 90, crossing into Wyoming. Approximately 11 miles west of Spearfish, take the exit to Beulah, Wyoming. Turn right at the top of the exit ramp and left at the junction, driving through Beulah. Approximately one mile after exiting the interstate, you will come to a gravel road on the right. Turn onto the gravel road, which jogs north and west several times, crossing over Wyoming 111 and eventually becoming Forest Service Road 843.

Approximately 13 miles after exiting the interstate, you will enter Forest Service property; and after approximately 16¾ miles you will reach the entry road to Cook Lake. Follow the access road to the lake, turning right at the 'T' in the road. Drive past the picnic area, over the dam and then park at the trailhead parking area. You can fish the pools immediately below the lake or follow the hiking trail to get to the pools and runs farther downstream.

IRON CREEK LAKE

Iron Creek Lake is a popular destination for fishing and camping, especially with the local residents. It sits high in the mountains and was formed by a small dam built across Iron Creek in 1936 by the WPA. Many northern Black Hills residents caught their first trout on this lake when they were children. The lake is frequently stocked with hatchery-raised rainbow trout and is known to produce some big fish. A 26-inch rainbow trout was taken there recently.

The lake, although small, can be fished with a motorized boat, canoe, float tube or kick boat. It can also be fished from shore. Good shoreline spots include: the small bay on the north side of the dam; the corner of the lake on the south side of the dam; the shore on the southeast side of the lake especially in the morning or evening; and the place where Iron Creek enters the lake.

There is a small store on the lake, with a campground and a few rental cabins, as well as a small community of seasonal camper trailers, some of which seem to date back almost to the time the lake was dammed.

To get to Iron Creek Lake, drive to the junction of Main Street and Jackson Boulevard in Spearfish. Go west on Jackson Boulevard until you reach Jonas Street where you will turn right. Drive north on Jonas Street until you reach Oliver Street. Turn left on Oliver Street, driving past the lumber mill until you reach Forest Service Road 134, then turn left at the sign for Iron Creek Lake. It's a 12-mile drive to the lake from the junction of Oliver Street and FS 134.

An alternative route to Iron Creek Lake is to drive south of Spearfish through Spearfish Canyon on Highway 14A until you reach Savoy. At Savoy, turn right onto Forest Service Road 222 and drive a little under 6 miles until you reach a stop sign. At the stop sign turn right onto Forest Service Road 134, driving until you once again reach Forest Service Road 222, a little under 11 miles from Savoy. At Forest Service Road 222, turn left and drive for a little less than 1/2 mile where you will see a sign on your left for Iron Creek Lake. Follow the sign and drive up to the lake.

REAUSAW LAKE

Created by damming Hay Creek, Reausaw Lake is a tiny body of water located in a meadow in the northern Black Hills. It is stocked with rainbow trout and is a popular fishing location for area residents. The lake has silted in over time and is scheduled to be dredged soon, according to officials with the United States Forest Service. When the dredging occurs, fishing at the lake will be disrupted when it is bypassed and drained.

Reausaw Lake can be accessed from Spearfish by driving east on Interstate 90 for approximately 5 1/2 miles to the junction of Highway 85. Turn right onto Highway 85 driving through Deadwood to the junction of Highway 385. Turn left onto Highway 385, driving south for a little more than 7 1/2 miles where you will come to Nemo Road. Turn left onto Nemo Road and go about 4 3/4 miles, until you see the lake in a meadow on the south side of the road.

STRAWBERRY HILL POND

This fishing pond, located adjacent to the Strawberry picnic ground south of Lead, is a nice place to have a picnic and try your luck at catching the rainbow trout that are stocked there. The pond is located on the west side of Highway 385, down the steep hill from the communities of Deadwood and Lead.

To access Strawberry Hill pond from Spearfish, drive east on Interstate 90 for approximately 5 1/2 miles to the junction of Highway 85. Turn right onto Highway 85, driving through Deadwood to the junction of Highway 385. Turn left onto Highway 385, driving south for a little over four miles where you will come to a sign for the Strawberry picnic ground. Turn right and drive downhill until you reach the parking area next to the bathrooms. The pond is adjacent to the parking area.

The catch-and-release section of Rapid Creek below Pactola Dam.

The Central Black Hills

Rapid Creek • Castle Creek • Boxelder Creek •
Beaver Creek • Spring Creek • Slate Creek •
Little Elk Creek • Ditch Creek • South Fork of
Castle Creek • Beaver Creek (Pennington
County) • Canyon Lake • Lake Pactola •
Deerfield Lake • Mitchell Lake • Major Lake •
Newton Lake • Dalton Lake • Roubaix Lake

The central Black Hills are deceptive to the first-time visitor passing through the region, or to one who never ventures off the main roads. The highways gently roll through relatively flat, higher-elevation pine forests and, although they pass through some scenic areas, if you want to experience the wonders of earth and water, you must get off these roads and head for the region's mountain canyons. There you will see dramatic displays of near-vertical bands of schist, slate and quartzite, the effects of the earth's upheaval, or *rifting*, exposed by millions of years of erosion. In the lower elevations, there are incredibly hewn limestone canyons.

Amid this stunning geological scenery is an equally impressive array of wildlife. The howls of coyotes pierce the night only to be replaced by the bugle of elk in the morning. Deer are abundant, as are wild turkeys. Occasionally, mountain lions have been spotted in the remote areas of the region.

The streams and lakes of the Central Black Hills lie mostly in Pennington County, with the exception of Boxelder Creek and Roubaix Lake, just to the north in Lawrence County. The dominant river in the central Black Hills is Rapid Creek, which slices through the region, picking up Slate and Castle Creeks before it pours into Lake Pactola, the reservoir created by the damming of the creek. Rapid Creek returns to its natural state below the Lake Pactola dam, flowing through spectacular canyons until it reaches Rapid City where it is again dammed to form a small recreational lake—Canyon Lake. Below Canyon Lake, it winds lazily through a greenway lined with mature cottonwood and elm trees that once marked streets and yards. The greenway exists as a result of a great tragedy. In 1972, this peaceful creek burst out of its banks during a night of violent rain, killing 238 people as it ripped through Rapid City.

In addition to Lake Pactola—the largest lake in the Black Hills—there are a number of other man-made lakes in this central region. Two of these are Deerfield Lake, an impoundment of Castle Creek, and Sheridan Lake, an impoundment on Spring Creek. A half-dozen other lakes are scattered throughout the rest of the region, with sizes ranging from several acres to less than an acre.

Rapid City is the largest community in the Black Hills, and South Dakota's second largest city. On the eastern edge of Rapid City is Ellsworth Air Force Base, proud home of the B-1 bomber and thousands of Air Force personnel. The remainder of the central Black Hills is dotted with small communities packed with history. Hill City, Rochford, Silver City, and Mystic—a ghost town listed on the National

Register of Historic Places—are the remnants of the 1870s gold rush. Nemo, located northwest of Rapid City, was once a bustling community when it was the site of the sawmill for Homestake gold mine.

Some of the Black Hills' best fishing is in this central region. At the top of the list is Rapid Creek, which is loaded with brown and brook trout, as are sections of Castle, Spring and Boxelder Creek. There are tiny brook-trout streams throughout the area such as Beaver and Little Elk Creeks. The lakes in the region have been stocked with an abundant supply of hatchery rainbow trout, making them great family get-away destinations.

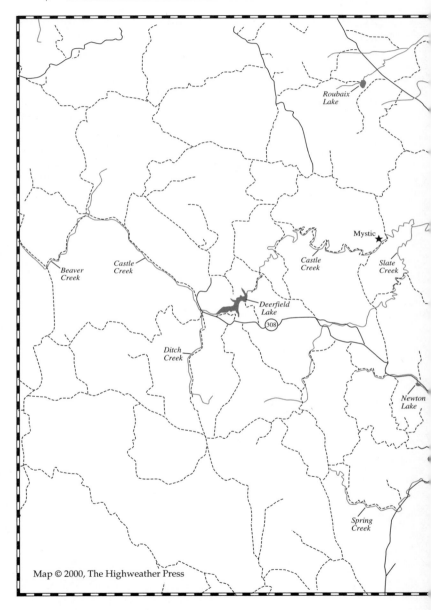

Roubaix
Lake

Mystic

Castle
Creek

Slate
Creek

Beaver
Creek

Castle
Creek

Deerfield
Lake

308

Ditch
Creek

Newton
Lake

Spring
Creek

Map © 2000, The Highweather Press

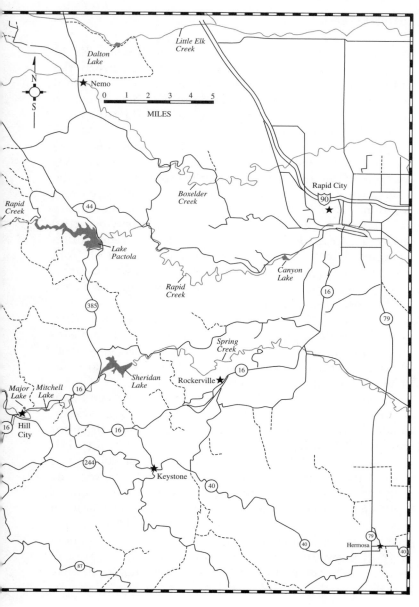

RAPID CREEK

Perhaps my favorite place to fish in the Black Hills is Rapid Creek. It is a diverse piece of water stretching nearly the entire width of the region. The creek is incredibly beautiful with sheer canyon walls and fast rolling water. It is also home to one of the highest populations of wild brown and brook trout in the Black Hills.

Rapid Creek has a long history of trout, having been the location of the first trout-stocking experiments by Hughes and Scott in the 1880s. It is also important historically for the Lakota because it was on this creek, probably at the current location of Rapid City, where the Lakota leader and military tactician, Crazy Horse, was born sometime between 1840 and 1845. Crazy Horse was responsible for orchestrating stunning defeats on the United States military, fresh from victory in the Civil War. He has been credited with creating a light military force which, at the time, was viewed as one of the most effective in the world.

As with Spearfish Creek in the northern Black Hills, trout fishing on Rapid Creek starts in town. The creek meanders through Rapid City, and there are good fishing spots throughout the city, with a couple of great ones no more than a few minutes drive from downtown.

To access the places to fish in town, follow Main Street west of downtown Rapid City until you reach Jackson Boulevard. Turn left onto Jackson Boulevard and drive for roughly 2¼ miles until you reach Meadowbrook Golf Course, which will be on your left. Turn into the golf course, park in the parking area at the clubhouse and walk onto the golf course and down to the creek. This is probably one of only a handful of golf courses in the United States that has a high-quality trout stream passing through it. This is a special regulation section of Rapid Creek and is known to hold a good population of wild brown trout. According to employees at the golf course, it is not uncommon to have people fish the creek early in the morning and then exchange their fly rod for their golf bag and play nine holes.

If the Meadowbrook clubhouse parking lot is full, there is another parking area just past the golf course on Park Drive. A few hundred feet down the street from the parking lot is a bridge that crosses Rapid Creek. From the bridge, the creek flows to the east through the golf course.

Another nice in-town location for trout fishing on Rapid Creek is upstream from Canyon Lake (p. 109)—an area that contains both wild and hatchery supplemented trout. You can access this location by parking in the lot on the northwest side of the lake and walk along the trail that runs upstream from Canyon Lake and behind the Cleghorn Springs Hatchery. As you walk up the trail, you'll begin to get a sense of the beauty of the Black Hills and Rapid Creek with high canyon walls rising up from the water's edge.

Upstream from the Cleghorn Springs Hatchery area, the fishing gets better and better. To access another good spot, follow Jackson Boulevard, which becomes Highway 44, west of Cleghorn Springs Hatchery. At this point you begin to climb up into the Black Hills and you can see the red siltstone and sandstone outcroppings of the foothills. To the south you can see the rugged canyons that Rapid Creek and its tributaries have created, including Dark Canyon.

Stay on Highway 44 for 5¾ miles from the Cleghorn Springs Hatchery until you come to a sign for the hamlet of Hisega. Follow the sign and turn left off of Highway 44. Drive approximately one mile, winding down into the canyon that Rapid Creek runs through, until you reach the hamlet of Hisega which was founded in 1908. In Hisega, there is a bridge that crosses Rapid Creek. You can fish downstream from the bridge or turn right after crossing the bridge and turn onto Toma Road, which runs adjacent to Rapid Creek for approximately ¼ of a mile. You can park on the streamside of the road and fish upstream.

To access the next location on Rapid Creek, drive west

from the Hisega turn off on Highway 44. The highway follows Rapid Creek upstream, crossing it several times. There are a number of bridges on the highway, which provide fishing access to Rapid Creek. Much of the property in this area is privately owned, so be respectful, and ask permission if you must cross private property.

Approximately five miles west of the Hisega turn off (10 ¾ miles from Cleghorn Springs Hatchery) is an access road for a location known as Placerville—a church camp on Rapid Creek. Follow the access road, which turns left off of Highway 44, winding through pines and hills until you reach the church camp, which will be on your left. At Placerville, turn right and the road will lead to a parking lot for a trailhead. There is a bridge that crosses Rapid Creek and a trail that runs upstream and downstream from the bridge.

Upstream on Rapid Creek from Placerville it is a special-regulation, catch-and-release-only section—one of my favorite places to fly fish in the Black Hills. It is also the favorite South Dakota trout fishing spot of Whit Fosburgh, the director of National Trout Unlimited's Coldwater Conservation Fund. Whit is a former member of the United States Flyfishing team and good friend of mine. It is beautiful trout water—filled with wild brown trout—slicing through steep canyons until it reaches the dam at Lake Pactola. Improvements have been made along much of this section of the creek to further enhance wild trout production—steps that have paid off.

Another way to access this catch-and-release section of Rapid Creek is to continue driving west on Highway 44 until you reach Highway 385, which is approximately 2½ miles from the Placerville turn-off. Turn left onto Highway 385 and drive south approximately 2 miles until you reach Pactola Basin Road, which is located on the top of the dam. Turn left onto Pactola Basin Road, and follow this steep, winding gravel road down to the canyon floor. Once on the floor of the canyon you will cross a small bridge over Rapid

Creek. Immediately after crossing the bridge, there are parking areas on both sides of the road. To access a parking area further downstream, continue driving straight-ahead on the road that crosses the small bridge. The road turns to the left, and approximately ¾ of a mile from the bridge, you will reach a parking area for the Tamarack Gulch Trailhead. From here you can fish upstream to the dam or downstream to Placerville.

The stilling basin itself is directly below the dam, which is to the right as you cross Rapid Creek on Pactola Basin Road. The basin is home to some huge fish, though the current regulations make this water catch-and-release only. The south side of the basin, where the main channel from the dam's tailwaters flows, is a good spot to fish, especially in the mornings and evenings. A float tube or a kick boat works well in the basin. This is also a good place to fish when Rapid Creek is running high or is heavily stained by runoff.

RAPID CREEK ABOVE LAKE PACTOLA

Fishing on Rapid Creek does not end at Lake Pactola. In fact, some of the creek's best fishing is on the stretch of water directly above the reservoir. To fish this section of Rapid Creek, follow Highway 44 west of Rapid City roughly 15 miles until you reach the junction of Highways 385 and 44. Turn right onto Highway 385 and drive north a little less than 1.5 miles where you will turn left at the sign for the hamlet of Silver City—named for the silver mines that existed in the area during the gold rush. Stay on this road for approximately 4.5 miles until you reach a bridge on your left that crosses Rapid Creek and takes you into Silver City. You can park here and fish downstream into Lake Pactola or upstream along the stretch of road that continues west. This is a fairly heavily fished (and stocked) section of the creek

A second location to fish in the area is along the Silver City Trail. To get there, drive past the bridge into Silver City for approximately ½ mile until you reach the parking area for the Silver City Trailhead. Park at the trailhead and walk upstream. You will encounter an incredibly beautiful section of Rapid Creek. An old railroad grade, converted into a hiking trail, follows the creek as it winds past jagged rock walls, pines, aspens, ferns, fields filled with wild flowers and abandoned mine shafts. Many stream improvements have been made in this area, which is home to a population of wild brown trout, and you can spend a day or days fishing this stretch of the creek. Fish all the way to where Slate and Castle Creeks join Rapid Creek—roughly four miles from the trailhead—an area known to hold some large trout.

There are a few more good places to fish on upper Rapid Creek near the town of Rochford. To get there, take Highway 44 west of Rapid City until you reach the junction of Highways 385 and 44. Turn right at the junction, and go approximately 4¼ miles until you reach the Rochford turnoff. Turn left and drive approximately 6½ miles until you reach Mystic Road. Turn left onto Mystic Road and you will come to a bridge a few hundred feet down the road. You can fish upstream on the south side of the creek or downstream, using the Mickelson Trail for access.

The next good places to fish on Rapid Creek are west and north of Rochford. To get to these spots, continue driving west on the Rochford Road (also known as Forest Service Road 231) past Mystic Road for approximately 4½ miles until you reach Rochford. Along the way, you may see an occasional gold panner on this stretch of Rapid Creek, which has been supplemented with hatchery trout due, in part, to the acidic content of the water.

Drive through Rochford veering to your left and approximately ¾ mile west of town you will reach South Rochford Road on your left where you can park and fish upstream or continue a little more than ½ mile further down Forest Service Road 231, where the road swings sharply to the left. There is parking at this location on the right side of the road adjacent to the Mickelson Trail. Beneath the footbridge for the Mickelson Trail, Rapid Creek splits upstream into the north and south forks. The George S. Mickelson Trail follows the north fork, providing easy access to wild brown- and brook-trout fishing, via foot or mountain bike. The further north you go, the better the fishing gets. Some of the land adjacent to this stretch of trail is privately owned so watch for signs prohibiting access.

Forest Service Road 231 continues to run parallel to the south fork of Rapid Creek, which contains wild brown and brook trout. (The south fork actually runs west.) To access this section of the creek, continue driving past where Rapid Creek splits for approximately ½ mile until you reach a meadow on the left side of the road. Park at the meadow and fish downstream, or upstream until you reach private land. You can also continue driving west on Forest Service Road 231 for approximately 7 miles until you reach Black Fox campground where you can fish both upstream and downstream.

While in the area, a trip into Rochford is worth your time. Founded in 1878 during the Gold Rush, it is home to 25 citizens (on a good day) and the infamous Moonshine Gulch Saloon. Little changed over its decades of operation, the saloon has an eclectic collection of Black Hills personal memorabilia hanging from its walls and ceilings.

Castle Creek

Castle Creek earned its name when the Custer Expedition marched into its upper reaches past mountain spires that, to members of the expedition, looked like the ramparts of castles. Upon entering the Castle Creek valley, from what is now Wyoming, a member of the expedition wrote in his journal that it was "luxuriantly rich and grassy with a fine stream running through it." Even though there were no trout in Castle Creek at the time, another member of the expedition referred to the creek and its tributaries as "trout brooks."

The lower reaches of Castle Creek start at an authentic ghost town called Mystic. Originally named Sitting Bull, Mystic was founded in 1876. It was a railroad center, the site of mines and a sawmill that operated until 1952. The last passenger train came through town in 1947, and the last freight train rolled through in the fall of 1983. The town is now on the National Register of Historic Places and several well-worn structures from the original community are still standing.

To get to Mystic, which Castle Creek flows through, drive to the junction of Highways 385 and 44 which is approximately 15 miles west of Rapid City near Lake Pactola. Drive north on 385 toward Deadwood for a little more than four miles until you reach the turnoff for Rochford Road (County Road 312). Turn left onto the Rochford Road and drive west for approximately 6½ miles until you reach Mystic Road.

Turn left on Mystic Road and drive approximately 3 miles where you will come to a sign for Mystic. There will be an old church on your right. Turn left onto George Frink Drive (named for the former sawmill that operated in the town) and drive a couple of hundred feet to a parking lot in front of one of Mystic's original structures. You can fish upstream and downstream at this point where there are both wild and hatchery planted trout. A hiking trail, the George S. Mickelson Trail, follows Castle Creek in both directions for easy access up and down the creek.

You can also drive further up Castle Creek by taking Mystic Road to the west of Mystic. The road runs parallel to the Creek and, for roughly a mile out of Mystic, there are several spots to pull over and fish. The Creek is very narrow at this point with lots of overhangs, so fishing can be challenging.

My favorite section of Castle Creek is below the dam. To

get there from Mystic, drive west on the Mystic Road, passing through Castleton—an old mining center—until you reach Deerfield Lake Road, approximately 8½ miles. Turn right on Deerfield Lake Road and drive for a little less than 4¾ miles until you reach Slate Prairie Road, which is marked with a sign for the Lazy S Campground. Turn right on Slate Prairie Road and after you have driven down the road for roughly a mile, look behind you to see one of the best views of Harney Peak—the highest mountain east of the Rocky Mountains. It is the granite mountain with the stone fire tower on its peak.

Continue driving down Slate Prairie Road approximately four miles from the Deerfield Lake Road junction, at which point you will reach Castle Creek valley. There is a parking area on the left. You can fish upstream or downstream at this location. It is roughly two miles upstream until you reach the Deerfield Dam and fishing on this stretch gets better the closer you get to the dam. Downstream, where fishing is also very good, you can fish for about a mile until you reach a church camp. Skirt around the church camp (they like to reserve the waters for the kids who attend the camp) and continue fishing downstream.

There are wild brook trout and brown trout on this stretch of Castle Creek and it is usually not heavily fished, especially during the week. One late Sunday afternoon, when most of the streams in the Black Hills were high and heavily stained and nearly unfishable, this section of Castle Creek was very fishable and I was the only person fishing on perhaps four miles of water. Another time I was fishing on this same stretch of water on a weekday morning, and the only other people fishing were a guide and his client.

There is a private campground with showers and electrical hookups a quarter mile further down Slate Prairie Road road. Approximately ¾ mile beyond the campground you will climb out of Castle Valley and onto a huge grassland known as Reynolds Prairie. It was originally named Elkhorn Prairie by the Custer expedition when they came

97

across an 8- to 10-foot-high stack of intermingled elk horns supported by three teepee poles. There is a stereo photograph of the stack of horns at the Journey Museum's Custer expedition display in Rapid City.

An alternate route to the section of Castle Creek that runs below the dam is to drive west out of downtown Rapid City on Main Street until you reach Jackson Boulevard. At Jackson Boulevard, turn left and drive approximately one mile until you reach Sheridan Lake Road. Turn left onto Sheridan Lake Road and drive for approximately 16½ miles (passing Sheridan Lake on your left) until you reach Highway 385. Turn left on Highway 385 and drive south to Hill City. As you drive into Hill City, turn right onto Deerfield Lake Road, which is directly past the junction of Highways 385 and 16. Stay on Deerfield Road for a little less than 10 miles until you come to Slate Prairie Road. At Slate Prairie Road, follow the above directions.

CASTLE CREEK ABOVE DEERFIELD LAKE

Castle Creek can also be fished above Deerfield Lake. Though the creek is tiny here, it is an excellent brook trout fishery that also includes some brown trout as well as hatchery planted rainbow trout that move up from Deerfield Lake. To get to this section of the creek, continue driving down Deerfield Road past the Slate Prairie Road turnoff for a little less than 6¼ miles. You will pass Deerfield Lake and the access points for the federal campgrounds on your right, eventually coming to the point where the creek enters the lake. You can fish Castle Creek upstream from the lake; there is an area to park near the footbridge that crosses the creek as it enters the lake. Roughly a quarter mile further upstream is Ditch Creek Road on the left. Fishing is good at the confluence of Ditch and Castle Creeks.

A little less than ½ mile beyond Ditch Creek Road on

Deerfield Road is another parking area on the left. You can fish at this location or continue driving a little further up the road where you will see a sign for Castle Creek. Turn left at the sign onto West Deerfield Road and there will be three parking areas on your left for fishing within a 1½ mile drive. The creek is so narrow at this point that you can jump across in most places, but the fishing here and further upstream is very good.

Castle Creek's relationship with history is very significant on this last stretch of water. When you are there, take a moment to look around you. The rock-capped mountains and buttes you see to the north are the mountains that inspired the Custer expedition to give the creek its name. Custer camped along this stretch of the creek on July 26 and 27, 1874. There is a stereo photographic plate in the South Dakota archives taken by the photographer who accompanied the expedition. He set up his tripod on one of the ridges above the creek and took a photograph of the wagons and horses and tents and men that filled this winding section of Castle Creek. In the photograph, you can see every twist and bend of the creek you are fishing.

BOXELDER CREEK

Boxelder Creek (sometimes written as "Box Elder Creek" on old roadsigns) is a popular stretch of trout water that flows between Rapid City and the hamlet of Nemo, through some of the more spectacular limestone gulches in the central Black Hills. The creek begins roughly six miles west of Nemo, where it is created by the confluence of three small streams—Coral, North Boxelder and Middle Boxelder Creeks. A fourth stream, South Boxelder Creek, also flows into the creek a couple of miles west of Nemo. Boxelder Creek and its tributaries hold healthy populations of wild brook trout as well as wild and hatchery-planted brown trout.

To access Boxelder Creek, follow Main Street west out of downtown Rapid City until you reach West Chicago Street where you will turn left. West Chicago Street turns into South Canyon Drive, which in turn, eventually becomes Nemo Road. Drive up into the Black Hills on Nemo Road, past the remnants of a forest fire and the red sandstone that marks the outer edge of the Black Hills.

Approximately 8½ miles after turning onto West Chicago Street, you will come to a meadow. On the left side of the road you will see a small fence that surrounds a rock and a white military grave marker. It is the grave of Private James King of H Troop 7th Cavalry who died of dysentery during Custer's exploration of the Black Hills. He died on August 13, 1874, and was laid to rest where he died, at the site of the expedition's last camp in the Black Hills.

Farther along Nemo Road, you'll descend a beautiful limestone canyon and cross a bridge over Boxelder Creek. At a distance of less than 10¼ miles from the junction of West Chicago and Main Street in Rapid City, you'll come to a parking area on the right where the limestone cliffs meet the creek. Fishing is good downstream and upstream from the parking area, as well as in the area directly below the cliffs.

The next area to fish is approximately 1 mile further up the road—11 miles out of Rapid City. There is a parking area on the left side of the road. Huge boulders, which have dropped into the streambed creating pools and a tiny waterfall, mark the stream at this location.

As you continue up Nemo Road, Boxelder Creek runs parallel to the road, flowing under it several times. Much of the land along this stretch of the creek is privately owned so ask permission before you cross private land to fish.

The next good spot to fish Boxelder Creek is approximately 14½ miles after turning onto West Chicago Street. You'll come to a sign indicating a sharp curve in the road.

Immediately after the curve, and before the bridge, you'll see a wooded area to the right with a primitive access road that runs downstream along the creek. You can park and fish upstream at this location, or drive up the road approximately a quarter of a mile to Steam Boat Rock picnic area, named for the rock mountain that towers over the creek at 5,081 feet. Park at the picnic area, which is a popular and fairly heavily fished section of Boxelder Creek, and fish up or downstream. There are several large pools below the cliffs at the upstream end of the picnic area that are good fishing.

There are also a couple of good places to fish on Boxelder Creek to the west of Nemo. When you reach Nemo, turn left off of Nemo Road onto a gravel road and drive past the store, which will be to your right after making the turn. You'll come to a bridge that crosses the creek. Cross the bridge and continue driving for approximately ½ mile and you will come to a small parking area on the left. You can park and fish upstream or downstream. A quarter of a mile further up the road you will pass the site where the 1970 White House Christmas tree was harvested. Approximately 1¼ miles after crossing the bridge behind the Nemo store, you will come to another good fishing area on the right where Boxelder Creek flows below a granite canyon wall.

One more place to fish is at Boxelder Forks U.S. Forest Service campground, which is a little less than 1¾ miles from the Nemo Bridge. South Boxelder Creek flows into Boxelder Creek from the southwest just below the bridge at the campground and there is a hiking trail that follows this tributary upstream. The further you hike up South Boxelder Creek, the better the wild brook trout fishing gets.

Spring Creek

Spring Creek, only a short drive from Rapid City, is popular with fly-fishers and non-fly fishers alike. The creek rises in the southern Black Hills, where it is fed by a number of tiny creeks and springs. It runs parallel to Highways 16 and 385 until it flows into Sheridan Lake. From Sheridan Lake, it tumbles down through a steep canyon and flows out of the Black Hills onto the western plains. The creek has populations of wild brook and brown trout, as well as hatchery supplemented brown trout.

In the past, Spring Creek below Sheridan Lake had a struggling wild fishery due, in large part, to the fact that the outlet structure at the lake was located at the bottom of the reservoir, sending oxygen-depleted water down the creek. Improvements have been made to the reservoir's release system and, according to officials with the South Dakota Department of Game, Fish and Parks, the changes have resulted in an increasing number of wild brown trout in the creek.

Curiously, the first three areas to fish on Spring Creek are each marked by a pair of bridges. To get to these locations, drive west out of downtown Rapid City on Main Street until you reach Jackson Boulevard. At Jackson Boulevard turn left and drive approximately one mile until you reach Sheridan Lake Road. Turn left onto Sheridan Lake Road and drive up into the Black Hills. As you follow this road, you will see the red sandstone outcroppings that characterize the outer reaches of the Black Hills.

Approximately 11½ miles from the intersection of Sheridan Lake Road and Jackson Boulevard you will descend a hill and, at the bottom of the hill, see two bridges in the road. Spring Creek flows beneath the bridges. There is a parking area on the right and you can fish upstream or downstream.

The next fishing area is approximately ½ mile further

down Sheridan Lake Road from the first stop. You will again come to two bridges that cross Spring Creek. There is an area where you can park on the right hand side of the road that is located between the two bridges.

Approximately one-half mile further down Sheridan Lake Road you will come to a third pair of bridges. There is a picnic area to your left as you cross the second bridge. There is a small parking lot at the picnic area. You can fish downstream or upstream toward the dam, which is roughly 1½ miles upstream.

One of my favorite places to fish on Spring Creek is at the Upper Spring Creek Trailhead for the Centennial Trail. The access road for the trailhead is located on the left side of the road approximately 13¾ miles from the intersection of Sheridan Lake Road and Jackson Boulevard. Turn left onto the access road and drive a little more than ¼ of a mile until you reach the parking area for the trailhead. During periods of high water, the tiny creek that flows past the turnoff of Sheridan Lake Road fills its banks, making it necessary to park, wade across the creek, and then follow the road down to the trailhead and Spring Creek. Once you reach the creek, you can fish upstream to the dam, which is one of the best stretches of water on lower Spring Creek.

Another way to reach this section of Spring Creek is at the Sheridan Lake dam itself. To do that, continue driving down Sheridan Road a couple of miles past the Upper Spring Creek Trailhead until you come to a sign for the Black Hills National Forest's Dakota Point picnic ground. (If you reach the exit for the Sheridan Lake north access recreational area you've gone too far.) Turn left at the sign for the picnic ground and follow the road for less than a ½ mile until you see a parking area on the left for the trailhead for Centennial Trail. Park at the trailhead and follow the trail down to the spillway for roughly ½ mile, staying to your right the entire way (the trail forks once). Walk over the footbridge at the spillway and follow the trail over the earthen dam. (You will see Spring Creek in the canyon to your left as you cross the dam.) When you reach the other side of the dam you will see a trail to your left that goes downhill. Follow the trail down to Spring Creek. This is a fairly strenuous hike, particularly in hot weather, so use your judgment. However, this stretch of Spring Creek is where I witnessed the largest caddis hatch I have ever seen in the Black Hills.

SPRING CREEK ABOVE SHERIDAN LAKE

Upstream from Sheridan Lake, Spring Creek flows roughly parallel to Highway 385/16. The road follows the creek upstream through Hill City to a few miles below the turn-off to Mt. Rushmore, where the creek veers to the west. While much of the land adjacent to the creek in this region is privately owned, there are a few good locations for accessing the creek. The upper section of the creek contains both wild brown and brook trout as well hatchery supplemented brown trout.

The first place to reach the creek is where Spring Creek flows into Sheridan Lake. To get to this spot, turn left at the junction of Sheridan Lake Road and Highway 385/16. Drive south for approximately 1½ miles, passing Sheridan Lake on your left, until you reach the entrance road for the lake's south campground. Turn onto this road and park on the right prior to the bridge that crosses the creek. You can fish upstream until you reach private property.

The next good place to fish on lower Spring Creek is south of Hill City. From the junction of Deerfield Road and Highway 385/16 on the north side of Hill City, drive south approximately 4¼ miles, past the road to Mt. Rushmore, until you reach Zimmer Ridge Road, which will be located on your right. Park on the shoulder of the highway and walk down to the access for the Mickelson Trail. Take the trail on the right until you reach the second footbridge. You can fish upstream at this point, although fishing is challenging because of the streamside growth, or continue up the trail to where the creek runs through a meadow.

The third good location to fish Spring Creek south of Sheridan Lake is approximately 6 miles south of the junction of Deerfield Road and Highway 385/16 in Hill City. At this location, turn right off of Highway 385/16 onto Spring Creek Road. In less than ¼ mile you will come to a bridge that crosses Spring Creek. Park at the bridge and fish upstream, or continue driving down Spring Creek Road for another ½ mile until you reach a meadow on your left where there's a primitive parking area.

SLATE CREEK/SLATE DAM

Slate Creek rises in the hills southeast of Deerfield Lake and flows toward Lake Pactola. Fed by a series of springs and small feeder creeks, it eventually flows into upper Rapid Creek west of Silver City. It contains both wild and hatchery planted brown trout and brook trout.

One of my favorite places to fish on Slate Creek is the section below the Slate Dam. (Above the dam is a four-acre lake that the South Dakota Department of Game, Fish and Parks stocks with rainbow trout. This small impoundment is heavily silted and earmarked for dredging.) Because of its isolated location, this section of the creek is not as heavily fished as the Black Hills streams that are closer to state highways. The roads to this spot are often rough, particularly in wet weather, but worth the trip both for the fishing and the wildlife. I once saw an elk calf standing next to the road, watching me curiously as I drove by within a few feet of it.

There are several ways to get to the section of Slate Creek below the dam. The first is to drive west out of downtown Rapid City on Main Street until you reach Jackson

Boulevard. At Jackson Boulevard, turn left and drive approximately one mile until you reach Sheridan Lake Road. Turn left onto Sheridan Lake Road and drive for approximately 16½ miles, past Sheridan Lake, until you reach Highway 385. Turn left onto Highway 385 and drive south for a little more than 5¼ miles until you reach China Gulch Road, which is also known as Forest Service Road 249. The road is located on the right, directly across Highway 385 from a motel.

Turn right onto China Gulch Road and drive for a little less than 6 miles—passing the road to Whisper Creek Ranch on your left—until you come to the junction of Forest Service Roads 249 and 350. Veer left onto Forest Service Road 350 and stay on that road, eventually passing a dilapidated log cabin on the right. At a little less than 10 miles from Highway 385 you will come to the Slate Dam. You can park at the dam and fish there or downstream. You can also continue down the Forest Service Road but, after you pass the dam, the road gets rougher.

An alternate route to this section of Slate Creek, which involves less time on Forest Service Roads, is via Hill City. To take this route, continue driving on Highway 385 past China Gulch Road until you reach Hill City. As you drive into Hill City, turn right onto Deerfield Lake Road (also known as County Road 308) which is directly past the junction of Highways 385 and 16. Stay on Deerfield Lake Road for a little less than 5¼ miles until you reach Mystic Road. Turn right onto Mystic Road and drive a little more than 3¼ miles until you reach Forest Service Road 530, also called Horse Creek Road. Turn right onto Forest Service Road 530 and after a little more than 1½ miles you will pass through a meadow and Slate Creek will be to your right. At a little more than 2¼ miles from Mystic Road, you will reach Slate Dam where you can park and fish downstream.

LITTLE ELK CREEK

This little creek offers some of the best wild brook trout fishing the central Black Hills has to offer. Flowing into and out of Dalton Lake, the creek tumbles down through Little Elk Canyon where it goes through a series of small drops and pools. A hiking trail provides easy access from where the creek flows out of the eastern Black Hills, upstream toward Dalton Lake.

To access Little Elk Creek from the Rapid City area, drive northwest on Interstate 90 approximately 12½ miles from exit 57 (also known as the Mt. Rushmore exit). Take exit 44, turn left at the bottom of the exit ramp and drive under the Interstate bridge, where you'll find the service road. Turn right onto the service road, and drive a little more than ¼ of a mile to the road to Little Elk Canyon. Turn left and drive for approximately 1½ miles until the road ends. Start fishing upstream from the dead-end.

An alternate way to access Little Elk Creek is by fishing downstream from the Dalton Lake Dam. For driving directions, consult the section on Dalton Lake.

DITCH CREEK/SOUTH FORK OF CASTLE CREEK

Ditch Creek and the South Fork of Castle Creek are two small creeks that join and eventually flow into Castle Creek directly above Deerfield Lake. They contain wild brook trout and rainbows. Some of the rainbows are planted; others enter the creek system from Deerfield Lake.

One of the best locations to fish is where the creeks join Castle Creek. To get there, drive west of Hill City on Deerfield Road for a little more than 16¼ miles from the junction of Highway 385, passing Deerfield Lake on your right, until you reach Ditch Road. Turn left onto Ditch Road and park immediately after you turn. The confluence of the creeks will be directly west of where you park. You can also fish upstream on the South Fork of Castle Creek from here.

To fish other locations on these two creeks, continue driving south a little less than a half mile after turning onto Ditch Road. You'll find an area on the right side of the road to park and fish up or downstream. Another spot is where Ditch Creek runs through a small meadow, a little more than 3¼ miles from turning onto Ditch Road. A third good place to fish is at the Ditch Creek campground, roughly four miles from the Ditch Road turnoff.

BEAVER CREEK (SOUTH DAKOTA)

Beaver Creek, in western Pennington County, has to be one of the best places to camp and fish in the Black Hills. It is extremely remote, sitting on the Wyoming border at approximately 6,200 feet, and contains a healthy, aggressive population of wild brook trout. The primitive campground located on the bank of the creek is pristine, as is the Natural Resource Management Area that surrounds the area.

To get to Beaver Creek, drive west of Hill City on Deerfield Road (located on the north side of town where it intersects with Highway 385) for a little more than 17 miles, passing the turnoffs to Mystic, Slate Prairie Road and Deerfield Lake. You will eventually reach West Deerfield Road, where you will turn left, following Castle Creek. Approximately 8¾ miles from the West Deerfield Road turnoff, you will come to the junction of Forest Service Roads 117 and 110. Drive straight ahead on FS 110, passing the turnoff to Cold Creek, until you reach the sign for Beaver Creek and Forest Service Road 109, which is a little more than 13½ miles from the West Deerfield Road junction. Turn onto FS 109 and drive for approximately 1¾ miles until you reach the junction of FS 109 and 111. You can park at the junction, where there are fence ladders, or *stiles*, and fish downstream. Or, turn right and drive to the campground. Park here and fish upstream.

CANYON LAKE

Canyon Lake is set in a beautiful city park on the western edge of Rapid City, and is a small impoundment of Rapid Creek. To access Canyon Lake, follow Main Street west of downtown Rapid City until you reach Jackson Boulevard. Turn left onto Jackson Boulevard and drive for roughly 2¼ miles, passing Meadowbrook Golf Course, which will be on your left. Continue driving on Jackson Boulevard for approximately ¼ mile past Park Drive. Turn left onto Canyon Lake Drive and then into the parking lot immediately to the right. (If that parking lot is full, there are others around the lake.)

Canyon Lake is stocked with hatchery trout including huge brood trout from the nearby hatchery. Trout in the six- to twelve-pound range frequently are caught in the lake, and it is where the state record brown, weighing more than 24 pounds, was caught. You can fish from shore, from the fishing piers on the lake, or with a float tube, canoe or kick boat. The park around the lake is a perfect place for an afternoon of trout fishing and a family picnic.

LAKE PACTOLA

Built in the 1950s to supply the water needs of Rapid City and Ellsworth Air Force Base, Lake Pactola is the Black Hills' largest lake. Approximately 15 miles west of Rapid City, the lake has 13¾ miles of shoreline, several campgrounds and boat launches. Wildlife is abundant throughout the area and you can often hear elk bugle in the mornings and coyotes howl at night. The lake was named for the town of Pactola, which was flooded when the reservoir was created and now lies on the bottom of the lake.

At one time, Lake Pactola was stocked with as many as 200,000 rainbow fingerlings each year by the Department of Game and Fish. The Department shifted their policy, however, and is currently putting in 40,000 to 60,000 catchable rainbow trout (8- to 10-inches) each year. It is a popular trout lake for residents of the Black Hills and tourists alike. Large rainbows are frequently caught there, as are lake trout, which were once stocked in the lake. The state record lake trout came out Lake Pactola.

In general, the best fishing on Lake Pactola is early in the morning or in the evening, and you'll often see people fishing from shore at those times of the day.

One good spot to fish is the bay at Veteran's Point. To get there, drive west of Rapid City on Highway 44 until you come to the junction of Highway 385. Turn left on Highway 385 and at approximately 1½ miles you will see the lake and a parking area for Veteran's Point on your right. A trail from the parking area will lead you down to a bay.

Another good location to fish from the shore is to stay on Highway 385 driving south past Veteran's Point. Cross the dam and as soon as you pass the visitor's center, turn right onto Custer Gulch Road, which will lead you toward a series of federal campgrounds. The first large bay on your right on Custer Gulch Road has several areas where you can park and hike down to the water.

If you want to fish the area where Rapid Creek flows into the Lake, turn right at the junction of Highways 44 and 385, driving north on Highway 385. Drive approximately 1.4 miles and turn left at the sign for Silver City. Drive on the Silver City road for a little less than 4½ miles until you reach a bridge that crosses Rapid Creek and takes you into Silver City. You'll see Lake Pactola on your left. Park near the bridge and hike down Rapid Creek to the lake.

DEERFIELD LAKE

Deerfield Lake is a 414-acre reservoir that lies on the western side of the Black Hills. It is named for the small hamlet of Deerfield, which was relocated in the 1940s to make way for the construction of the dam and reservoir. Originally called Mountain City, Deerfield was founded during the Black Hills Gold Rush of the 1870s.

Not surprisingly, Deerfield Lake is a place few residents of the Black Hills have ever visited. It's fairly isolated and is not on the way to any major community or tourist destination, other than the State of Wyoming. And at 5900 feet it is often cold, even in the summer.

Deerfield Lake was created by the damming of Castle Creek in 1947, to provide water for Rapid City and Ellsworth Air Force Base. It is the second largest lake in the Black Hills, with Lake Pactola being the largest. Deerfield is known by those who visit as a good place for camping, boating, hiking and fishing.

Like Pactola, Deerfield Lake is aggressively stocked each year by the South Dakota Game and Fish with approximately 120,000 rainbow trout fingerlings. The lake also holds splake—a brook trout/lake trout hybrid—which were planted because of the lake's cold temperature and because of the rapidly growing sport-fishing interest in the fish. The lake is home to some large trout, and has produced a state-record brook trout of more than 8 pounds, and a state-record splake weighing in at more than 10 pounds.

There are several good places to fish on Deerfield Lake that do not require the use of a boat. To fish the lake, drive west out of downtown Rapid City on Main Street until you reach Jackson Boulevard. At Jackson Boulevard, turn left and drive approximately one mile until you reach Sheridan Lake Road. Turn left onto Sheridan Lake Road and drive for approximately 16½ miles, past Sheridan Lake, until you reach Highway 385. Turn left on Highway 385 and drive to

Hill City. As you drive into Hill City, turn right onto Deerfield Lake Road, which is directly past the junction of Highways 385 and 16. Stay on Deerfield Road for a little more than 19 miles, until you come to a sign for Gold Run trailhead. Turn right into the trailhead parking area and you can fish in that bay. (Highways 385 and 16 can also be accessed driving west from Mt. Rushmore.)

For the next couple of miles beyond Gold Run Trailhead on Deerfield Road, you will pass access areas for the federal campgrounds and picnic grounds located on the south side of the lake. Many of the bays can be accessed along here, and are particularly productive in the mornings and evenings.

One of the most popular and productive spots on Deerfield Lake is on either side of the point where Castle Creek flows into the lake. To reach this spot, stay on Deerfield Road a little less than 2¼ miles past the Gold Run trailhead. You will see the lake on your right and there is parking on the right shoulder of the road. There is also a parking area near the footbridge that crosses Castle Creek as it enters Deerfield Lake. At this point you can also follow Castle Creek, or you can fish up Ditch Creek and the South Fork of Castle Creek, which flows into Castle Creek from the south a quarter mile or so upstream from the Lake.

MITCHELL LAKE & MAJOR LAKE

Many people, including area residents, drive by these two central Black Hills lakes without knowing that they are indeed lakes. They're so small, in fact, they could pass for large natural pools in a creek. The two lakes, which are on opposite sides of Highway 385/16 near Hill City, are only a couple of miles apart and were created by damming small creeks.

The lakes are popular fishing locations for their ease of

access and because of the large trout that are stocked in them, as attested to by the pictures in the local tackle shops. The lakes are often used for local youth fishing derbies. Spring Creek, one of the popular trout fishing creeks in the central Black Hills, flows into and out of Mitchell Lake.

To fish either lake drive west out of downtown Rapid City on Main Street until you reach Jackson Boulevard. At Jackson Boulevard turn left and drive approximately one mile until you reach Sheridan Lake Road. Turn left onto Sheridan Lake Road. Stay on Sheridan Lake Road until you pass Sheridan Lake (approximately 16½ miles) and reach the junction of Highway 385 and Sheridan Lake Road. Turn left onto Highway 385. Drive south for approximately 5 miles and you will see Mitchell Lake on the left. There is parking adjacent to the lake on the left side of the road.

To fish Major Lake, continue south on Highway 385/16 past the Black Hills Forest Information Center until you enter Hill City. Krull's market will be on your left and on the right will be a sign for Ranger Field. Turn onto the road for Ranger Field and within a block you will reach the lake.

NEWTON LAKE

Newton Lake, located a few miles northwest of Hill City, is so tiny you can literally cast across it. It exists because of a small impoundment on Newton Fork Creek. The South Dakota Department of Game, Fish and Parks stocks the lake, and the creek contains a decent population of wild brook trout. It's a fun little lake to fish, especially where the creek enters it and upstream from the lake on the creek. There is a small picnic area at the lake as well.

To fish Newton Lake, follow the directions for getting to Deerfield Lake. Newton Lake is on the left side of the road three miles northwest of the junction of Deerfield Lake Road and Highway 385 in Hill City.

DALTON LAKE

Of all of the lakes in the Black Hills, Dalton Lake is probably my favorite for camping and trout fishing. It is in a fairly isolated area of the Black Hills and it has about a dozen primitive Forest Service campsites at its edge. On several occasions when I have camped there during the week, I have been the only one at the lake.

The damming of Little Elk Creek created Dalton Lake. It is only a few acres in size but it has a healthy population of wild brook trout and hatchery planted rainbow trout.

In addition to its remote location, quiet setting and great trout fishing, Dalton Lake has a couple of other benefits. The first is Little Elk Creek, which offers great wild brook trout fishing. There is also a trailhead for a hiking trail near the dam. The trail will take you up into some scenic areas of the eastern Black Hills.

To reach Dalton Lake, drive west on Main Street out of downtown Rapid City until you reach West Chicago Street. Turn left on West Chicago Street, which becomes South Canyon Drive and eventually Nemo Road. Stay on Nemo Road, and drive up into the Black Hills, passing the remnants of the forest fire and the limestone canyons that mark Boxelder Creek. If you are interested, there are several areas to stop and fish along Boxelder Creek on your way to Dalton Lake. (See section on Boxelder Creek.)

Approximately 18 miles from the junction of Main and Chicago Streets in Rapid City, you'll come to the town of Nemo. Continue past Nemo on Nemo Road for approximately ½ mile and you will see a sign for the road to Dalton Lake. Turn right onto this road and after approximately four miles you will see a second sign for Dalton Lake. Turn right at this sign onto a gravel road that will take you down to the lake. As you are driving on this final stretch of road, look to your left and you will see some of the spectacular granite outcroppings that distinguish Little Elk Canyon.

Note: Dalton Lake has slowly been silting in over time and is currently proposed for dredging which will disrupt fishing when the lake is drained and bypassed. However, as of this writing, the dredging has not been scheduled.

ROUBAIX LAKE

Roubaix Lake with its population of hatchery planted rainbow trout, campgrounds and picnic areas is popular with families. It was created when Middle Boxelder Creek was dammed. It's frequently the site of local fishing derbies, and the entire lake is easily accessed for fishing. Some of the more popular fishing spots are on either side of the dam and where the creek enters the lake. There is also a good population of wild brook trout both downstream and upstream from the lake on Middle Boxelder Creek. (Portions of the Middle Boxelder Creek pass through private property so ask permission if you plan to fish more than a quarter of a mile up or downstream from the lake.)

Roubaix Lake can be easily accessed from either the northern or central Black Hills. To get there from Rapid City, drive west on Highway 44 out of Rapid City until you reach the junction of Highway 385. At Highway 385 turn right heading north for a little over 10 miles and you will reach the entrance for the lake on your left.

From the Deadwood-Lead area, go to the junction of Highways 385 and 85. Drive south on 385 for almost 13 miles and you will reach the entrance to Roubaix Lake on your right.

Note: Like Dalton, Roubaix is slowly silting in and is under consideration for dredging. While a dredging date has not been set as of this writing, when it does occur, fishing will be disrupted for a while when the lake is drained and bypassed.

The dramatic beauty of a southern Black Hills stream.

THE SOUTHERN BLACK HILLS

FRENCH CREEK • GRACE COOLIDGE CREEK •
IRON CREEK • BATTLE CREEK • BISMARCK LAKE •
STOCKADE LAKE • LEGION LAKE • CENTER LAKE •
LAKOTA LAKE • SYLVAN LAKE • HORSETHIEF LAKE

If you've ever seen a picture of the Black Hills, chances are it was taken somewhere in the southern Black Hills. Mt. Rushmore. Harney Peak. The jagged granite spires of the Needles. Buffalo wandering in the grasslands of Custer State Park. The granite one-lane tunnels of Iron Mountain Road framing Mt. Rushmore. All of these features—and more—are in the southern Black Hills. And in between these incredible acts of nature and man are small picturesque lakes filled with rainbow trout and historic streams that snake their way through wilderness areas and past herds of buffalo and elk, and are filled with brown and brook trout.

The southern Black Hills regions lies entirely within Custer County of South Dakota, with Custer State Park as the dominant feature. The park, which encompasses 73,000 acres, gets its name from the fact that the Custer expedition established their base camp on French Creek for about a week in 1874, and were the first non-Indians to explore the park's now famous features. Created in 1919 to protect the unique natural resource aspects of the region, the park quickly became a national attraction.

From its beginning, Custer State Park has played a role in American history. In 1927, president Calvin Coolidge came to the Black Hills to spend a vacation in the newly created park. He was so enamored of the area that his visit lingered beyond the scheduled three weeks and he eventually stayed the entire summer, turning the Custer State Park Game Lodge into his summer White House. During his stay, Coolidge made the startling decision not to seek a second term of office.

While in the park, Coolidge spent much of his time fly-fishing on the creeks, and wound up taking to the sport. His success was probably inflated due, in part, to the fact that officials from the federal hatchery had heavily stocked the creek for his benefit, and that the stocking included some of their huge brood stock.

Coolidge is not the only President to have fished in Custer State Park. Dwight Eisenhower came here too, after a tour of Ellsworth Air Force Base outside of Rapid City. He spent three days at the Game Lodge in June of 1953, during which time he fished for brook trout. Eisenhower, an avid, almost fanatical, fly-fisherman, reported that the fishing was excellent.

North of Custer State Park are the Needles and Cathedral Spires, radical granite outcroppings that are a rock climber's dream and easy to access thanks to the scenic Needles Highway. High above the Needles is the 7,242-foot Harney Peak. An old stone lookout tower, once used for fire spotting, sits on the peak.

The Harney Peak fire tower contains the ashes of Dr. McGillycuddy, a physician and the first non-Indian to climb Harney Peak. McGillycuddy attended Crazy Horse as he lay dying at Ft. Robinson with a bayonet wound through his back. The presence of his remains is marked with a plaque at the fire tower that has the inscription, "Wasicu Wakan," or mystical white person—the Lakota term for a white doctor.

In the eastern shadow of Harney Peak lies the Black Elk wilderness area, named for Black Elk, a famous Lakota holy man. The Needles, Harney Peak and the wilderness area are all linked by a series of hiking trails.

To the south of Custer State Park is Wind Cave National Park, nearly 30,000 acres of mixed prairie and pines. A wildlife and natural resource marvel, the park sits on top of one of the largest caves in the United States. Only an estimated ten percent of the cave has been mapped, making it one of the truly unexplored places in the United States.

The dominant trout water in the southern Black Hills is French Creek, a small stream that has its beginnings west of the town of Custer. The creek flows through a 12-mile gorge, including a section known as the "narrows" in Custer State Park. That section of the creek is a protected natural area, and truly one of the most spectacular places to fish for wild brown trout in the Black Hills. The park is also home to Grace Coolidge Creek as well as Bismarck, Center, Legion and Sylvan Lakes. The lakes are adequately stocked with hatchery raised rainbow trout in the 8- to 10-inch range.

To the north of Custer State Park are Lakota Lake and Horsethief Lake. There are also a handful of small streams with brook trout in this region including Iron, Grizzly and Battle Creeks.

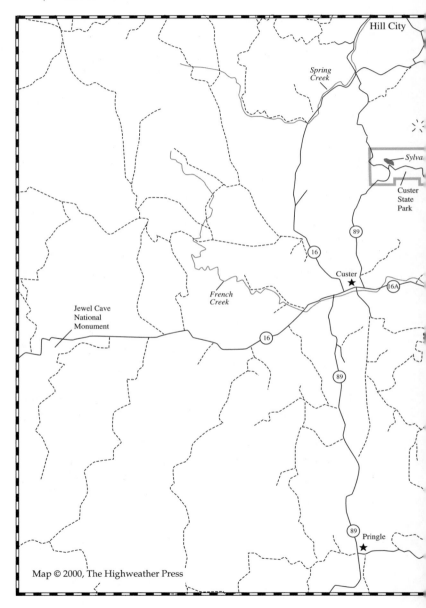

Hill City

Spring Creek

Sylva

Custer State Park

89

16

Custer

16A

French Creek

Jewel Cave National Monument

16

89

89 Pringle

Map © 2000, The Highweather Press

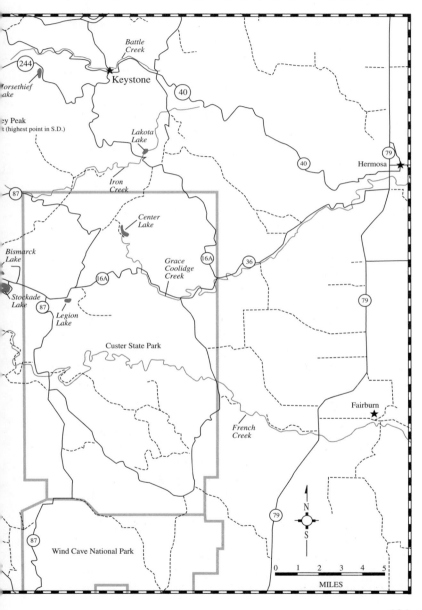

FRENCH CREEK

This small creek, which winds its way through the southern Black Hills, changed forever the relations between the American Indians of the Upper Great Plains and the United States government. It was here, directly to the east of present-day Custer, South Dakota, where George Armstrong Custer's contingent camped for a week in 1874, and here where gold miners accompanying him discovered gold. The news set off a flood of fortune seekers into the Black Hills. Only later, much too late for the Lakota and the Cheyenne, was it reported that the Custer expedition's gold discovery was greatly exaggerated, and in reality amounted to little more than a couple of grains of gold.

Gold or no gold, French Creek is beautiful. East of Custer, in the vicinity of the Custer expedition's camp, it winds through a meadow bordered by massive granite outcroppings. It flows south out of Stockade Lake and then turns east into Custer State Park where it flows through a portion of the park that has been designated a natural area because of its isolated, undisturbed beauty. There, the creek flows through a narrow gorge, so narrow in places you have to wade in the stream to pass through the area. Near the eastern edge of the natural area, the creek performs an incredible act of nature—it disappears into a sinkhole only to reappear later. From the natural area, it flows downward, out of the Black Hills and onto the Plains where it eventually joins the Cheyenne River.

French Creek, particularly within the French Creek Natural Area, is known for sizable, crafty wild brown trout and there are several locations that allow for fairly easy access to good fishing.

From the junction of Highway 385 and Main Street in Custer, drive east on Highway 16A passing a replica of the Gordon Stockade on the right. The stockade is where a group of squatters came seeking gold the year after Custer's expedition, only to be evicted by the United States government. Stay on Highway 16A for approximately 6½ miles until you reach Highway 87. Turn right onto Highway 87 passing Mt. Coolidge on the right and the remnants of the 1988 Custer State Park fire. Approximately 4 miles from the Highway 87 turnoff, you will come to a picnic area on the right where there is parking and a footbridge. This is a popular fishing area for park visitors and there are several nice pools downstream from the picnic area that have been stocked with trout.

Continue east on Highway 87 for approximately ½ mile past the picnic area and you will pass Blue Bell Lodge, built by an executive with the Bell Telephone Company in the early 1920s as a retreat. Just past Blue Bell Lodge on the left you will see horse barns and, just beyond the horse barns, a sign for French Creek Natural Area. Follow the sign, which will put you on Custer State Park Road 4. Stay on this road for approximately 2¼ miles until you reach the Custer State Park Horse Camp. You can park at the Horse Camp and fish upstream through the meadow where there are both wild and stocked trout, or continue a little more than a ¼ mile beyond the Horse Camp to the parking area for the French Creek Natural Area trailhead. The primitive trail follows French Creek, crossing it several times. Fishing for wild trout gets better and better downstream from the trailhead.

If you want to see what only a small percentage of park visitors experience, grab a backpack, sleeping bag and tent and hike into the natural area, fishing until you come to one of the two backpack campsites. The trail through the natural area is approximately a twelve-mile hike one way and there are trailheads on each end. If you are planning an overnight hike in the natural area, contact Custer State Park to make sure there is space at one of the campsites. The telephone number is listed in the appendix.

There is also a way to access the center of the French Creek Natural Area without hiking its full length. To do that, follow the above directions to Custer State Park Horse Camp. Directly past the camp, you will veer to the right onto Custer State Park Road 4 and stay on that road for a little less than 3 miles until you come to Custer State Park Road 5. Turn left onto Custer State Park Road 5 for 1¼ miles until you come to Custer State Park Road 2 where you will turn left. (Note: this section of Custer State Park Road 2 can be impassable for most vehicles in wet weather.) Stay on Custer State Park Road 2 for a little more than one mile where you will veer to the right eventually coming to a turn-around area on the edge of the woods designated by small blue metal diamonds that have been attached to some of the trees. Park here and follow the diamonds, which will guide you on a primitive trail down to the creek. There is a healthy population of wild brown trout in this stretch and fishing is excellent both upstream and downstream from this access point. It is a fairly strenuous climb both down to the creek and back up to the parking area so use your judgement.

Accessing French Creek from the east side of Custer State Park

The French Creek Natural Area—as well as the eastern trailhead for the French Creek Trail—can be accessed from the east side of Custer State Park. To try this route, drive east out of Custer on Highway 16A until you reach the Custer State Park Game Lodge, approximately 13 miles from the junction of Highway 385 and Main Street in Custer. Drive a little less than ¾ of a mile east of the Game Lodge where you will come to a sign for the Wildlife Loop and the park's airport. Turn right onto this road and follow it for a little less than 3 ¾ miles to where you drive down a hill. A small sign on your right marks the eastern trailhead for the French Creek Trail. (If you come to a bridge crossing French Creek you've gone too far.) Turn right onto the access road for the trailhead and follow it until it ends at a parking area. It is approximately a two-mile hike to the campsite and fishing is good beyond that point.

To get to the center of the French Creek Natural Area

from the east, continue driving on the Game Loop Road, past the access point for the eastern trailhead for the French Creek Trail, until you come within sight of the Custer State Park Wildlife Station—a stone and log building. Just before the Wildlife Station you will come to Custer State Park Road 5. Turn right onto this road and stay on it for a little more than two miles until you come to Custer State Park Road 2. Turn right onto Custer State Park Road 2. Stay on Park Road 2 for a little more than a mile where you will veer to the right, eventually coming to a turn-around area near the edge of the woods, designated by small blue metal diamonds that have been affixed to the trees.

Whether you are fishing French Creek for a couple of hours while having a family picnic or backpacking into the natural area, there are several precautions to keep in mind. The first is rattlesnakes, which are fairly common along portions of the creek. The second is poison ivy, which is in abundance. The third are buffalo, which roam wild throughout the park and can be aggressive if you approach them, especially if they are with calves. Finally, there are elk that, especially during the fall, can be aggressive. For me, these features make fishing on French Creek a very special place.

GRACE COOLIDGE CREEK

Named for the former First Lady who, with her husband, made the Custer State Park Game Lodge her summer White House in 1927, Grace Coolidge Creek is a popular fishing spot for local fishing enthusiasts as well as tourists. The creek tumbles out of Center Lake into a series of pools created by several small dams, and then through a well-traveled area of Custer State Park, marked by the Game Lodge. The creek contains wild brook trout and stocked rainbow trout.

A hiking trail, with trailheads at Center Lake and Highway 16A, follows the creek, crossing it several times. It's roughly a three-mile hike each way, and well worth taking the time to venture along its entire length with a fishing rod in hand—both for the size of some of the trout you will encounter as well as the beauty of the hike.

The creek and pools near the trailheads are fairly heavily fished. However, like many Black Hills streams, the further you hike in along Grace Coolidge Creek, the fewer people you're likely to encounter. Fishing in the area of the third dam from the Highway 16A trailhead and upstream from there can be particularly good.

To access the Highway 16A trailhead, at the junction of Highway 385 and Main Street in Custer, drive east on Highway 16A/89. After you pass the vestiges of the Custer State Park forest fire, you'll come to the Grace Coolidge Walk-in Fishing Area Trailhead on the left, approximately 11½ miles from Custer. There is parking at the trailhead, across the road from the Grace Coolidge Campground.

To fish Grace Coolidge Creek from the Center Lake Trailhead, start at the junction of Highway 385 and Main Street in Custer, go east on Highway 16A for a little less than 8 miles, and you will come to the Highway 87 turnoff for Center Lake on the left. Drive north on Highway 87 for a little less than 3 miles until you reach the turnoff on the right for the Black Hills Playhouse and Center Lake. (Approximately one mile north of the turnoff from Highway 16A you will pass an interesting photo exhibit on the left, showing photographs of the valley from Custer's 1874 expedition and from today.) Turn right onto the Playhouse/Center Lake Road until you come to the sign for the Center Lake campground entrance. Drive through the camping area, following the signs for the beach. When you reach the beach, which will be on the left, the trailhead will be at the end of the road right beyond the beach showers. Follow the trail uphill for a short distance and then it will descend to Grace Coolidge Creek.

Grace Coolidge Creek downstream from walk-in area

Downstream from the Highway 16A Trailhead, Grace Coolidge Creek continues to wander through Custer State Park, flowing along Highway 16A through a number of camping and cabin areas. This is a very popular fishing area for families and tourists visiting the park as the creek is, literally, just a few steps from the porch of the historic Game Lodge. It is stocked along this stretch because of the heavy fishing pressure.

To fish Grace Coolidge Creek in this area, drive a little less than a quarter mile past the trailhead on Highway 16A until you reach the Grace Coolidge Tent Area on the left, where the Creek runs beneath a sheer rock wall. There is parking in the Tent Area, or you can drive further downstream to the Fish Hook Picnic Area, which is a little less than a mile from the Highway 16A trailhead. There is a small impoundment at the picnic area and you can fish both upstream and downstream from the impoundment. Half a mile beyond the Fish Hook Picnic Area is the Coolidge General Store on the right where you can park and fish the creek, which flows downstream from the store through a meadow and back across Highway 16A near the Game Lodge.

BATTLE CREEK

Battle Creek is passed by millions of tourists each year on their way to Mt. Rushmore. The creek, which contains wild brook trout, converges with Grizzly Bear Creek in Keystone—a tourism center in the central Black Hills. One fairly productive section of Battle Creek lies, literally, between a parking lot and a highway. The creek is worth stopping by to try a little brook trout fishing on your way to French or upper Spring Creek, or if you are spending the night at one of Keystone's motels

To access the creek, drive west on Main Street in Rapid City until you reach Mt. Rushmore Road, also known as Highway 16. Turn left onto Mt. Rushmore Road, driving south for a little less than 17 miles until you come to the junction of Highways 16 and 16A. Turn left onto Highway 16A and approximately 20 miles from Main Street in Rapid City you will come to Keystone and a stoplight at the junction of Highway 40.

Turn right at the stoplight onto Old Hill City Road and drive for approximately 1 mile until you come to a parking area on the left side of the road with a culvert beneath it that Battle Creek runs through. You can fish upstream from this point, where there are a number of small pools, until the creek crosses the highway. Another location to fish on this stretch of Battle Creek is 1 mile further down Old Hill City Road at Laferty Gulch Road. Park at the junction and fish downstream. Like many Black Hills brook trout streams, this section of the creek can be challenging fishing with lots of overhangs and streamside growth.

To fish the "parking lot" section of Battle Creek, turn left at the junction of Highways 16A and 40 and drive approximately 1 mile until you reach 3rd Street. Turn right into the large parking lot and fish the creek upstream.

IRON CREEK

Iron Creek is a small stream on the southeast corner of the Peter Norbeck Wildlife Preserve. (Norbeck, a former South Dakota Governor, played a critical role in creating Custer State Park and in preserving the area's natural resources.) The creek was dammed to form Lakota Lake.

The creek contains wild brook trout, and stocked rainbow and brown trout. There is a hiking trail that follows Iron Creek upstream from the southwest end of Lakota Lake, making easy access for about a two-mile stretch of the creek. You can also reach the creek downstream from Lakota Lake, via the dam and spillway.

To fish Iron Creek, follow the directions to Lakota Lake by taking Highway 16A east out of Custer, past the Custer State Park Game Lodge, until you reach the junction of the Custer State Park Wildlife Loop and Highway 16A, a little less than 14 miles from the junction of Highway 385 and Main Street in Custer. Turn left at the junction and stay on Highway 16A for just a little less than 11 miles, where you will come to a sharp left-hand curve in the road. Within that curve, you will see a sign for Lakota Lake on the right. As soon as you enter the access road, Iron Creek will be on the right. You can park on the shoulder of the road and fish upstream from the lake or continue on the access road until you reach the large parking area. The dam is located on the northeast corner of the lake.

BISMARCK LAKE

This small lake is overshadowed by its larger neighbor, Stockade Lake, which lies just across the highway. The lake gets so little attention that few Black Hills residents can tell you precisely where it is. That fact translates to less fishing pressure than some of the better-known trout lakes, such as Legion, Center and Sylvan. Like other area lakes, Bismarck is stocked with rainbow trout. Fishing can be quite good in the bay where the boat ramp is located, or next to the dam and spillway.

To reach Bismarck Lake, at the junction of Highway 385 and Main Street in Custer drive east on Highway 16A for approximately 4½ miles passing Stockade Lake on the right. The entrance to Bismarck Lake is on the left. Turn in at the entrance road and follow the signs to the lake access area.

STOCKADE LAKE

Stockade Lake is the largest lake in the southern Black Hills. It was created by the damming of French Creek, and also receives the overflows from its neighbor to the north, Bismarck Lake.

Stockade Lake was named for the Gordon Stockade, which stood on French Creek approximately at the location where the lake is today. The Gordon Stockade was built by twenty-six residents from Sioux City, Iowa who illegally entered the Black Hills upon hearing the Custer expedition's reports of a gold discovery on French Creek. The party included a woman and a nine-year old boy and they spent Christmas and the winter of 1874 at this location until they were discovered and evicted by the U.S. cavalry.

The Gordon Party were the first known white settlers in the Black Hills and the action of the United States Government to evict them in compliance with the treaty they had signed with the Lakota, was the first and last effort to physically remove treaty violators from the region. Within a year after the Gordon Party was evicted, thousands of gold seekers poured into the Black Hills, establishing camps and even towns. The gold stampede was on and their presence forever changed the Black Hills.

Like the Black Hills, Stockade Lake has evolved as a fishery. While once primarily a trout fishing lake, it now contains bass, pike and even bullheads. While the South Dakota Department of Game, Fish and Parks is currently stocking the lake, a decision could possibly be made in the near future to stop the practice.

If you want to try your luck at fishing Stockade Lake, the best place to fish is where French Creek enters the lake. To get there drive east on Highway 16A from the junction of Highway 385 and Main Street in Custer. You will pass the Highway 89 turnoff, and the location of Custer's camp in 1874—commemorated by a historical marker.

Approximately three miles from the junction of Highway 385 and Main Street in Custer, you'll see the replica of the Gordon Stockade on your right. There is a parking area near the stockade, which stands near the point where the creek enters the lake.

LEGION LAKE

Legion Lake is a small, man-made lake, about halfway between Custer and the Custer State Park Game Lodge. It was created when Galena Creek was dammed, and named for an American Legion Post that once leased the land where the lake is now. The Legion Lake Lodge and resort, operated by the Custer State Park Resort Company, is located at the lake.

In addition to being well stocked with trout by Game and Fish, the lake offers swimming and a variety of watercraft rentals. There are a couple of fishing docks at the north end of the lake, and a swimming beach on its east side. The lake provides easy access, via a hiking trail, to the Badger Hole, the log cabin home of Charles "Badger" Clark, a famous cowboy poet.

The lake is a popular fishing destination for tourists and locals alike. A hiking trail around the lake can be used to access the entire shoreline. A couple of the better spots to fish include the area near the fishing docks where Galena Creek enters the lake, and on either side of the spillway on the southeast corner of the lake.

To find Legion Lake, drive east on Highway 16A from the junction of Highway 385 and Main Street in Custer, past the entrance to Custer State Park and Stockade Lake. At a little less than 7¼ miles, the lake will be on your right. There's a parking area on the right side of the road near the fishing docks. Park there or at the Legion Lake Lodge.

CENTER LAKE

Center Lake is a small lake in Custer State Park, next to the Black Hills Playhouse, a long-running professional summer theatre. It is popular for its camping—it boasts the largest number of campsites of any of the Custer State Park lakes. It is also a popular fishing spot, both in the lake as well as downstream in Grace Coolidge Creek, which was dammed to create Center Lake.

While trout fishing is good on most of Center Lake due, in large part, to the South Dakota Department of Game, Fish and Parks' rainbow trout-stocking program, one of the better locations is on its northwest end where Grace Coolidge Creek enters the lake. You can also fish the creek upstream from the lake where there's a small population of wild brook trout.

To reach Center Lake, drive on Highway 89A east from the junction of Main Street and Highway 385 in Custer. Drive a little more than 7¾ miles passing Stockade Lake and Legion Lake, until you reach Highway 87. Turn left onto Highway 87. Stay on Highway 87 for a little less than 3 miles, passing the remnants of a forest fire on the right, until you reach the turnoff for the Black Hills Playhouse and Center Lake. (Staying on Highway 87 will take you through the Needles, eventually skirting Sylvan Lake.) Turn right onto the Playhouse/Center Lake Road until you come to the sign for the Center Lake campground entrance. Drive through the camping area and follow the signs for the beach, where there is parking.

LAKOTA LAKE

Lakota Lake is a small lake in the Norbeck Wildlife Preserve that is a popular fishing destination for Black Hills residents. Originally called Biltmore Lake, its name was eventually changed to Lakota, the proper name for the Plains Indian culture, also known as Sioux. (The word "Sioux" is a bastardized version of a term used by the Ojibwe—enemies of the Lakota in the 18th Century—to describe the Lakota. It means something along the lines of "Snake.")

Like many Black Hills lakes, Lakota is far too small for motorized boats. It is, however, a good lake for fishing with a float tube or kick boat, or simply from shore.

Currently, the South Dakota Department of Game, Fish and Parks is stocking Lakota Lake with rainbow trout, including some that are in excess of 15 inches. Size restrictions allow only trout in excess of 14 inches to be kept. There are also restrictions prohibiting the use of baitfish.

A couple of good spots to fish are on either side of the bay where Iron Creek enters the lake, which is to the right of the entrance road as you drive in. Other good locations are the bay on the west side of the lake (which is directly north of the lake's parking and picnic area) and the areas on either side of the spillway.

To access Lakota Lake, take Highway 16A east out of Custer, past the Custer State Park Game Lodge, until you reach the junction of the Custer State Park Wildlife Loop and Highway 16A, a little less than 14 miles from the junction of Highway 385 and Main Street in Custer. Turn left at the junction and stay on Highway 16A for a little less than 11 miles until you come to a sharp left curve in the road. Within that curve, you will see a sign for Lakota Lake, which will be on the right. Follow the access road to the parking areas.

An alternate route to Lakota Lake is to take Highway 16 south of out Rapid City until you reach the junction of Highways 16 and 16A. Take Highway 16A through Keystone, past the exit for Mt. Rushmore, over the remarkable "pigtail" bridge system, and then through a series of tunnels carved out of granite. The entrance to the Lakota Lake will be on your left roughly two miles past the third tunnel.

SYLVAN LAKE

One of the most beautiful and dramatic lakes in the Black Hills is Sylvan Lake. The lake lies at the base of Harney Peak and features massive granite outcroppings, which are reflected in the surface of the lake when the wind is calm. It is a tranquil experience to fish this lake early in the morning or on a still evening when the lake looks like glass, broken only by rising trout.

The lake was originally the site of one of the early Black Hills tourist hotels—the Sylvan Lake Hotel—which burned down in the 1930s. The Sylvan Lake Resort replaced the hotel, and its new location was suggested by the legendary architect, Frank Lloyd Wright. The resort is owned by the State of South Dakota and leased to private managers. It continues to be one of the Black Hills' finer lodges, and also includes cabins, as well as a restaurant with an incredible view of the Black Hills.

The state stocks Sylvan Lake regularly with rainbow trout. It is small enough to fish from shore and a trail provides easy access around the entire lake. A couple of the more popular locations to fish are the east side of the lake, directly east of the Sylvan Lake General Store, and in the small, sheltered bay on the north side of the lake.

In addition to fishing, there are a series of hiking trails with trailheads at Sylvan Lake including the trails to Harney Peak, the highest mountain in the continental United States east of the Rocky Mountains, and Cathedral Spires, a dramatic cluster of granite outcroppings.

To get to Sylvan Lake, start at the junction of Highway 385 and Main Street in Custer, and go east on Highway 89/16A for approximately ¾ miles until you reach the junction of Highway 89. Turn left onto Highway 89 and go a little more than 6½ miles, through the entrance to Custer State Park. Veer to your right when the road splits, and go through the park entrance station to the lake. You'll see the

Sylvan Lake General Store on the left. There is a parking area to the east of the store.

An alternate route to Sylvan Lake is to take Highway 385/16 south of Hill City for a little less than 3½ miles (from the Deerfield Lake Road) until you reach the junction of Highway 87. Turn left onto Highway 87, eventually passing though a tunnel and passing Sylvan Lake Resort on your left. At a little more than 5½ miles from the junction of Highways 385/16 and 87, you will come to the entrance station for Custer State Park. Sylvan Lake will be directly ahead of the entrance station.

HORSETHIEF LAKE

Horsethief Lake is a small, picturesque lake full of stocked rainbow trout. It lies at an elevation of 5,000 feet, in the shadow of Mt. Rushmore National Park, and has a campground with approximately three dozen campsites. It's a popular tourist destination because of its location and its fishing. Good places to fish include the bay at the spillway, which is adjacent to Highway 244, and the bay on the southeast corner of the lake.

To get to Horsethief Lake, drive north from Custer on Highway 16 for approximately 10½ miles until you reach the junction of Highway 244. Turn right onto Highway 244 and go a little more than 5¾ miles until you come to the Horsethief Lake campground exit on your right. Pull into and park in the campground or continue driving down Highway 244 until you see the lake on your right. There is a parking area between the highway and the lake.

Alternate access routes for Horsethief Lake include driving west of Mt. Rushmore on Highway 244 or by driving south of Hill City on Highway 16 until you reach Highway 244 where you will turn left and drive for 5¾ miles.

APPENDIX

The following list, sorted by regions, streams and lakes, is a select group of camping and lodging locations in the Black Hills. For additional locations consult travel directories or lodging guides.

NORTHERN BLACK HILLS:

Spearfish, Little Spearfish and Hanna Creeks:
Rod and Gun USFS Campground (800-280-2267)
Timon USFS Campground (800-280-2267)
Spearfish Canyon Resort (605-584-3435)

Iron Creek Lake and Beaver Creek:
Iron Creek Lake Campground (605-642-5851)

Beaver Creek—Wyoming and Cook Lake:
Cook Lake USFS Campground (800-280-2267)

Sand Creek—Wyoming:
Sand Creek State Campground (available on a first-come basis)

CENTRAL BLACK HILLS:

Rapid Creek and Lake Pactola:
Bear Gulch USFS Campground (800-280-2267)
Pactola USFS Campground (800-280-2267)

Upper Rapid Creek:
Happy Trails Cabins—Silver City (605-574-2177)
Black Fox USFS Campground (800-280-2267)

Castle and Ditch Creeks and Deerfield Lake:
Lazy S Campground (605-574-2649)
Dutchman USFS Campground (800-280-2267)
Whitetail USFS Campground (800-280-2267)

Custer Trail USFS Campground (800-280-2267)
Ditch Creek USFS Campground (800-280-2267)

Boxelder Creek:
Boxelder Forks USFS Campground (800-280-2267)
Nemo Guest Ranch (605-578-2708)

Little Elk Creek and Dalton Lake:
Dalton Lake USFS Campground (800-280-2267)

Spring and Slate Creeks, Sheridan, Mitchell, Major and Newton Lakes:
Sheridan South USFS Campground (800-280-2267)

Upper Spring Creek:
Oreville USFS Campground (800-280-2267)

Beaver Creek:
Beaver Creek USFS Campground (800-280-2267)

Robaix Lake:
Robaix Lake USFS Campground (800-280-2267)

Southern Black Hills:

French Creek:
Blue Bell Lodge and Resort (605-255-4531, reservations: 800-658-3530)
Blue Bell Campground (800-710-2267)
French Creek Natural Area (self-registration, for information call 605-255-4464)

Grace Coolidge Creek and Center Lake:
Custer State Park Game Lodge (605-255-4541, reservations: 800-658-3530)
Center Lake Campground (first-come basis)
Grace Coolidge Campground (first-come basis)
Game Lodge Campground (800-710-2267)

Sylvan Lake:
Sylvan Lake Resort (605-574-2561, reservations: 800-658-3530)
Sylvan Lake Campground (800-710-2267)

Legion Lake:
Legion Lake Lodge and Resort (605-255-4521, reservations: 800-658-3530)
Legion Lake Campground (800-710-2267)

Bismarck and Stockade Lakes:
Bismarck Lake USFS Campground (800-280-2267)
Stockade Lake Campground (800-710-2267)

Horsethief Lake:
Horsethief Lake USFS Campground (800-280-2267)

For Black Hills weather conditions:
Rapid City Office of the National Weather Service
300 East Signal Drive
Rapid City, SD 57701
605-341-7531
http://www.crh.noaa.gov/unr/index.htm

Stream flow conditions for certain Black Hills' creeks:
United States Geological Survey (USGS)
1608 Mt. View Road
Rapid City, SD 57702
605-355-4560
http://sv01dsdhrn.cr.usgs.gov/rt-cgi/gen_tbl_pg
or http://sd.water.usgs.gov/

For information on Black Hills tourist attractions and communities:
South Dakota Department of Tourism
711 East Wells Avenue
Pierre, South Dakota 57501
800-732-5682

Wyoming Division of Tourism
I-25 at College Drive

Cheyenne, Wyoming 82002
800-225-5996

Black Hills Badlands & Lakes Association of South Dakota
1851 Discovery Circle
Rapid City, SD 57701
Phone—605-355-3600, Fax—605-355-3601
http://www.blackhillsattractions.com/

BlackHills OnLine
511 W Jackson Blvd. Suite A
Spearfish, SD 57783
Phone—605-642-8166, Fax—605-642-1771
http://www.blackhills.com/

Flyshops:
Custom Caster
316 West Main
Lead, South Dakota 57754
Phone—605-584-2217
http://www.deadwood.net/custcast

Dakota Angler & Outfitter
516 7th Street
Rapid City, SD 57701
Phone—605-341-2450 Fax—605-341-1457
http://www.flyfishsd.com/

Scheels All Sports
Rushmore Mall
2200 North Maple
Rapid City, South Dakota 57701
Phone—605-342-9033

Sharp's Sporting Goods and
Sundance Mercantile
109 North 3rd
Sundance, Wyoming 82729
307-283-2274

For information on Black Hills fishing regulations:
Department of Game, Fish and Parks
523 East Capitol
Pierre, South Dakota 57501
605-773-3384

Wyoming Game and Fish Department
Regional Fisheries Supervisor
Box 6249
Sheridan, Wyoming 82801
307-672-7418

To report poaching or wildlife violations:
1-800-592-5522 (South Dakota)
1-800-442-4331 (Wyoming)

For information on Custer State Park:
Custer State Park
HC 83, Box 70
Custer, South Dakota 57730
605-255-4515
800-710-2267 (camping reservations)
http://www.state.sd.us/sdparks/

Custer State Park Resort Company
HC 83 Box 74
Custer, South Dakota 57730
800-658-3530 (resort reservations)
Fax-605-255-4706
http://www.custerresorts.com

For information on Black Hills trails:
Black Hills Trail Office
HC 37, Box 604
Lead, South Dakota 57754
605-584-3896

For copies of the South Dakota Campground guide:
South Dakota Campground Owners Association
P.O. Box 124
Keystone, South Dakota 57751
http://www.blackhills.com/sdcoa

*For Black Hills National Forest information including maps, trail
guides and campground reservations:*
Office of the Forest Supervisor
Black Hills National Forest
RR 2 Box 200
Custer, South Dakota 57730
605-673-22516   05-673-4954 (TTY)
800-280-2267 (campground reservations)

Bearlodge Ranger District
US 14 East, Box 680
Sundance, Wyoming 82729
307-283-1361

For information on Wind Cave National Park:
Wind Cave
RR 1, Box 190
Hot Springs, South Dakota 57747
605-745-4600

Trout-Fishing Organizations:
Trout Unlimited
1500 Wilson Boulevard
Suite 310
Arlington, Virginia 22209-2404
Phone—703-522-0200
Fax—703-284-9400
http://www.tu.org

Black Hills Fly-fishers
P.O. Box 1621
Rapid City, SD 57709

SELECTED BIBLIOGRAPHY

Crazy Horse, The Strange Man of the Oglalas, Mari Sandoz, University of Nebraska Press, 1961

D.C. Booth Centennial Booklet, Paul Higbee, 1996

Fly Fishing, Tom McNally, Outdoor Life—Harper and Row, 1978

Fly Fishing Equipment & Skills, John van Vliet, Creative Publishing International, 1996

Hiking South Dakota's Black Hills Country, Bert and Jane Gildart, Falcon Press Publishing Company, Inc., 1996

History of South Dakota, Herbert S. Schell, University of Nebraska Press, 1975

Legends of the Lakota, James LaPointe, The Indian Historian Press, 1976

Mato Paha: The story of Bear Butte, Thomas E. Odell, T.E. Odell, 1942

Prelude to Glory, Herbert Krause and Gary D. Olson, Brevet Press, 1974

Trout, Ray Bergman, Alfred A. Knopf, Inc., 1943

INDEX OF STREAMS AND LAKES

Trout Fishing